Research Your Surname
and Your Family Tree

Lewis Thomson Fisher Clarke Bailey Campbell Collins Ellis Allen Owen Mills Wilson Webb Matthews Simpson Hall

Find out what your surname means and trace your ancestors who share it too

Dr Graeme Davis

howto

D0273558

Published by How To Books Ltd,
Spring Hill House, Spring Hill Road,
Begbroke, Oxford OX5 1RX
Tel: (01865) 375794. Fax: (01865) 379162
info@howtobooks.co.uk
www.howtobooks.co.uk

How To Books greatly reduce the carbon footprint of their books by sourcing their typesetting and printing in the UK.

British Library Cataloguing in Publication Data
A catalogue record for this book is available from the British Library

ISBN: 978 1 84528 434 3

Cover design by Baseline Arts Ltd, Oxford
Produced for How To Books by Deer Park Productions, Tavistock, Devon
Typeset by PDQ Typesetting, Newcastle-under-Lyme, Staffs.
Printed and bound in Great Britain by Bell & Bain Ltd, Glasgow

NOTE: The material contained in this book is set out in good faith for general guidance and no liability can be accepted for loss or expense incurred as a result of relying in particular circumstances on statements made in the book. Laws and regulations are complex and liable to change, and readers should check the current position with the relevant authorities before making personal arrangements.

Contents

The Small Print

THE REGIONS OF THE BRITISH ISLES

In writing about the surnames of the British Isles I have needed to make frequent reference to areas within the British Isles. I have used the following conventions.

- I have treated the four home countries as England, Wales, Scotland and Ireland. The 20th-century division of Ireland has minimal impact on the surnames of Northern Ireland and the Irish Republic.

- I have used the established regional names for parts of England: South East, South West, East Anglia, East Midland, West Midlands, North East, North West.

- For England 'South' means South East + South West; 'Midlands' means East Midlands + West Midlands; 'North' means North East + North West. Additionally the East–West divide, sometimes important in surname distribution, leads to 'East' (South East + East Anglia + East Midlands + North East) and 'West' (South West + West Midlands + North West).

- For Wales I have used geographical terms for north, central and south.

- For Scotland I have occasionally used established regional names (particularly Borders) though for surname distribution the distinction most useful is often between Lowland and Highland following the traditional concept of the Highland Line.

- For all parts of the British Isles I have used traditional county names before the 1974 revisions. The old counties well reflect cultural and linguistic communities and therefore map the distribution of surnames far better than the post-1974 counties; indeed the artificial county constructions post-1974 are an example of cultural vandalism.

- For Ireland I have additionally used the four provinces of Ulster, Connaught, Leinster and Munster.

- The Channel Islands and Isle of Man are treated as discrete areas. Orkney and Shetland are sometimes treated separately as their naming practices frequently differ from other parts of Scotland.

- 'British Isles' is applied to the territory now occupied by the United Kingdom, Channel Islands, Isle of Man and the Irish Republic. This usage dates from antiquity and is very well established. The view expressed by many in the Irish Republic that the term 'Britain and Ireland' should instead be used has been rejected here as it excludes the Channel Islands and the Isle of Man. A term such as 'The Isles' is not so far generally accepted so I have not used it, but it is however a synonym for British Isles as here used.

THE SCOPE OF THIS BOOK

The concept of British Isles surnames has been interpreted within this book as the surnames established in the British Isles prior to 1945. This is the surnames of the Celtic and Germanic peoples of the British Isles, along with the surnames of Norman French, Romany Gypsy, Jewish and French Huguenot origin. The surnames brought to the British Isles by migrants during the last two generations or so are not within the scope of this book. These surnames are best understood within the culture from which they arise.

Welcome!

I do beseech you, chiefly that I may set it in my prayers, What is
your name?

William Shakespeare, The Tempest

The surname stock of the British Isles is an enormous cultural
treasure. Everyone who bears a British Isles surname has a
tangible link with the past. Understanding surnames – our own,
and those of our relatives, our friends and acquaintances – is a
part of understanding our British Isles heritage.

There was a time when people knew the reason why someone
had a particular surname. For every surname there was a point of
origin when someone adopted a surname for a reason and then
passed this name to their children. For some generations
following this point of origin the family would probably know
why they had a particular surname, and know what their
grandfather or grandfather's grandfather had done to gain the
surname. Yet with the passage of centuries this knowledge has
usually been lost. Finding this point of origin, this reason for a
particular name, is the reason for this book.

We are seeing a revolution in the ways in which we can study the
surnames of the British Isles. Databases crunch the mass of
information into something that is useful. Online sources are fast
growing and ever more informative. Genetic techniques offer

exciting new tools. What hasn't kept pace is the dictionaries which claim to give surname meanings or the countless companies that seek to sell a largely fictitious surname history. This book shows you how you can access the materials yourself to understand British Isles surnames.

The heritage of the British Empire means that surnames that had their birth in the British Isles are now found not only within the British Isles but also within those countries settled by colonists from the British Isles. In each country to which it has been carried, the British Isles surname system has been modified so that in nations including the USA, Canada, Australia and New Zealand we see developments of what is essentially the British Isles system. Much of these systems can be understood through the materials introduced by this book.

1

Understanding Surnames

In the British Isles we all have surnames. Indeed most of the world has them. This book shows you how to research surnames you are interested in, whether your own or other people's, both as a part of investigating a family tree and as an independent activity.

The emphasis of this book is on the journey, not the destination. Often it is possible to say that a surname comes from a particular part of the British Isles, was created in a specific century or even at a specific date, and that we can know what it first meant. Sometimes not all of this can be achieved, but understanding why it is not possible is in itself a step towards understanding a surname. This book aims to take you on the journey, to see what can or cannot be achieved. It stands in contrast to the great number of bogus claims about surname origins. Many dozens of companies promise to tell you (for a fee) the history of your surname, usually complete with coat of arms and often with presentation on an historic scroll, ready for framing. While it is occasionally possible that fragments of truth are within these sources, the vast majority are simply fiction. You can do a much better job yourself.

WHAT IS A SURNAME?

The bedrock of the naming system in the British Isles is the first

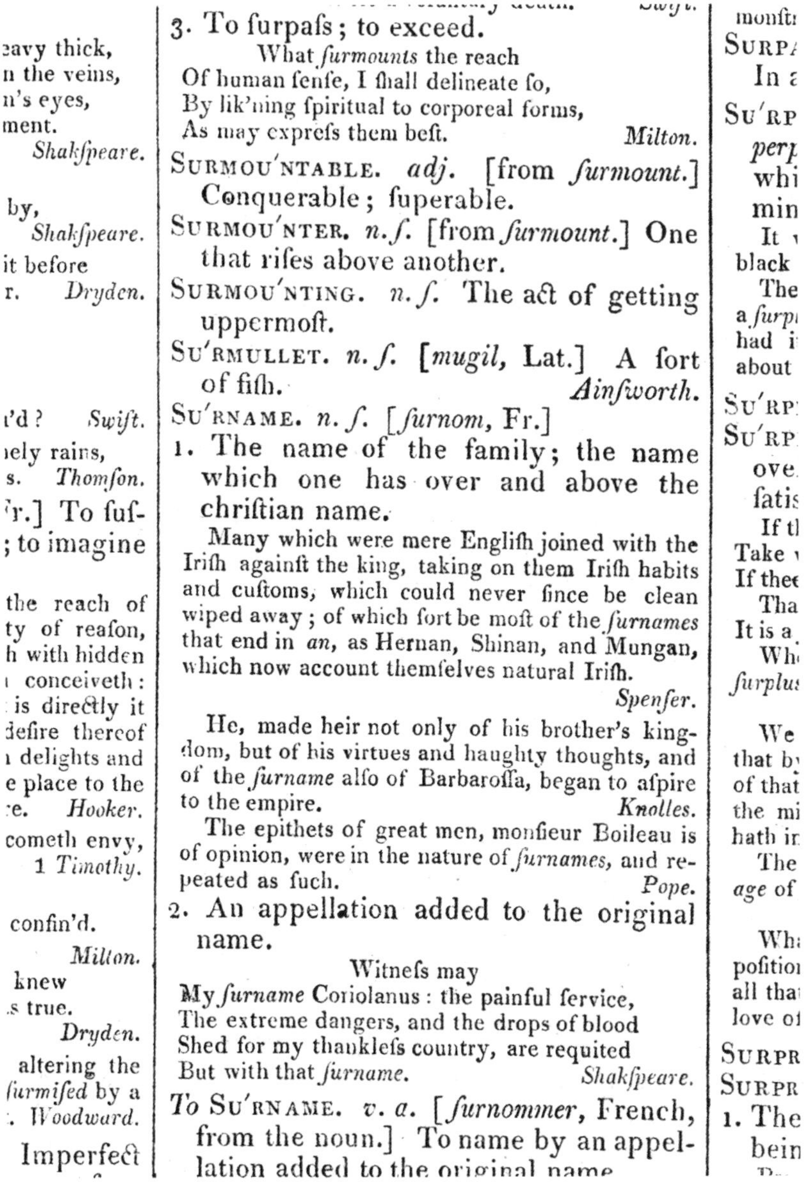

eavy thick,
n the veins,
n's eyes,
ment.
  Shakspeare.

by,
  Shakspeare.
it before
r. *Dryden.*

'd ? *Swift.*
iely rains,
s. *Thomson.*
'r.] To suf-
; to imagine

the reach of
ty of reason,
h with hidden
ı conceiveth :
is directly it
desire thereof
ı delights and
e place to the
:e. *Hooker.*
cometh envy,
  1 *Timothy.*

confin'd.
  Milton.
knew
s true.
  Dryden.
altering the
furmised by a
. *Woodward.*

Imperfect

---

3. To surpass ; to exceed.
      What *surmounts* the reach
  Of human sense, I shall delineate so,
  By lik'ning spiritual to corporeal forms,
  As may express them best.   *Milton.*

SURMOU'NTABLE. *adj.* [from *surmount.*]
  Conquerable ; superable.
SURMOU'NTER. *n.s.* [from *surmount.*] One
  that rises above another.
SURMOU'NTING. *n.s.* The act of getting
  uppermost.
SU'RMULLET. *n.s.* [*mugil*, Lat.] A sort
  of fish.   *Ainsworth.*
SU'RNAME. *n.s.* [*surnom*, Fr.]
1. The name of the family; the name
  which one has over and above the
  christian name.
  Many which were mere English joined with the
  Irish against the king, taking on them Irish habits
  and customs, which could never since be clean
  wiped away ; of which sort be most of the *surnames*
  that end in *an*, as Hernan, Shinan, and Mungan,
  which now account themselves natural Irish.
      Spenser.
  He, made heir not only of his brother's kingdom, but of his virtues and haughty thoughts, and
  of the *surname* also of Barbarossa, began to aspire
  to the empire.   *Knolles.*
  The epithets of great men, monsieur Boileau is
  of opinion, were in the nature of *surnames*, and repeated as such.   *Pope.*
2. An appellation added to the original
  name.
      Witness may
  My *surname* Coriolanus : the painful service,
  The extreme dangers, and the drops of blood
  Shed for my thankless country, are requited
  But with that *surname*.   *Shakspeare.*
To SU'RNAME. *v. a.* [*surnommer*, French,
  from the noun.] To name by an appellation added to the original name

---

monst
SURPA
  In a
SU'RP
  perƒ
  whi
  min
  It ᵥ
  black
  The
  a ƒurp
  had i
  about
SU'RP:
SU'RP.
  ove.
  satis
  If tl
  Take ᵥ
  If thee
  Tha
  It is a
  Whᵢ
  ƒurplu:
  We
  that bᵥ
  of that
  the mi
  hath iᵣ
  The
  age of
  Whᵢ
  position
  all thaᵢ
  love oі
SURPR
SURPR
1. The
  beiᵢ

Figure 1. What is a surname? For 18th-century lexicographer Samuel Johnson it is a name held 'over and above the Christian name'. For Alexander Pope surnames were 'the epithets of great men'.

name. In the early Middle Ages people had just one name; what we think of today as the given name or Christian name.

In the early Middle Ages a much greater range of first names was used than we use today. Nevertheless, often the need was felt to distinguish between two bearers of the same first name. This was done by use of a by-name, a descriptive add-on. Typically this was a statement of the lands the person owned, the place where they lived or their occupation. Sometimes it was a patronymic (someone's son) and more rarely a nickname. These by-names were used on occasions and for a purpose. One person might be known by several different by-names during their life, or known by a by-name only within a one-off, formal context. The person described by a by-name was unlikely to regard it as part of their name. Nor would a by-name pass to someone's children.

A surname is a development of a by-name which has the special characteristic of being passed on to children. It is a name held in addition to the first name – the sense of *surname* is 'super name', name held over and above the main name. The British Isles very early regularized the inheritance of surnames as passing from father to children, much as property was inherited.

WHERE DO SURNAMES COME FROM?

There are very few types of origin for surnames, both in the British Isles and in the rest of the world. In a nutshell, these are as follows.

■ Place names. These include both precise places as the name of a town or a village as well as what appear to be landscape or typographic features such as hill, river.

- Occupation names

- Patronymics

- Nicknames

Figure 2. Surname, autograph and photograph. These three key parts of our identity are combined in this 1912 photograph.

Of these, the place names are by far the most common, accounting for around half of the British Isles surnames. Occupation names and patronymics account for most of the rest, with nicknames being rare.

It is often difficult to decide which category a surname belongs to. Thus Mills may be a place name in origin – from any of countless place names which include the element 'mill'. It may be an occupation name, a miller. Or it may be a patronymic, the son of Miles. It may even be all three, with the name having arisen separately at least three times.

How old are they?

Surnames were an idea that came to the British Isles with the Norman Conquest. Most British Isles surnames were formed in the period 1066–1400. This may be regarded as the great age of surname formation in England, Scotland and Ireland – Welsh surnames are generally later. Surnames have been formed in every subsequent century. They have also been brought to Britain by centuries of migrants.

Very often we cannot quite identify the first bearer of a particular name, but rather a group of early bearers. An 18th-century description of the Douglas family applies equally well to the vast majority of British Isles surnames:

> We do not know them in the fountain but in the stream; not in the root but in the stock and stem, for we know not who was the first mean man that did raise...himself above the vulgar.
>
> Hume of Godscroft, *History of the House and Race of Douglas*, 1743

How do the British Isles compare with the rest of the world?

Surnames of similar types are found in most of Europe, and often the method of formation, age and means of transmission is remarkably uniform throughout the countries of Europe. Many of the concepts in this book apply also to these traditions.

Very many cultures do not have a tradition of surnames, though most of these have recently adopted them. Some countries do not use a surname tradition but a patronymic system, where individuals use their father's first name plus son or daughter.

Figure 3. Surname and business name frequently combine, as in shop names. This example is from Brighton, around 1950.

Some cultures have surname traditions much longer than any in the British Isles. While our earliest surnames are approaching their first millennium, China has surnames that are nearly five times that age. There, surnames were adopted by law in 2852 BC with the stated intent of preventing intermarriage. They are in the form of surname or clan name (almost always monosyllabic) followed by a generation number name and a personal name. The first two parts of the name were therefore inherited.

Figure 4. The Chinese character for Li, the world's most common surname.

ACTIVITY

Surnames of interest

▶ This book is a practical guide. It works best if you scribble down a list of half a dozen or a dozen surnames that you are interested in and explore with them the ideas presented here.

▶ Quite a few surnames – including the 50 most common – are discussed in one form or another in this book. You might find useful information here about a surname you are interested in.

▶ Of course you can check online sources or dictionaries of surnames at your local library. But be warned, the average quality is abysmal. They do at least offer a starting point for the journey of this book.

2

Finding out How Surnames Change

Most surnames in the British Isles have been around for six centuries. A few have been around for more than nine centuries. In perhaps two dozen generations they have been subject to extensive change. Certainly there are some surnames which are in the same form as when they arose, but most show changes, big and small. There is no simple process by which it is possible to deduce the original form from the present-day form.

SURNAMES AND DICTIONARIES

You may of course look up your surname in a surname dictionary. You might be lucky. The good news about the surname dictionaries is that they do have something to say about the most common surnames. Just 50 surnames cover around 20% of the UK population, and these are certainly in the dictionaries. Around 40% of the people of the British Isles have one of the 500 most common surnames. And 60% have one of the 1000 most common. Very many of the surname dictionaries do therefore cover a good percentage of the population.

But in terms of individual surnames a lot is left out. Data from the 2000 electoral register suggests there are just under half a million different surnames in use in the UK today. Many of these have been brought to the UK by migrants post-1945 (and so are outside the scope of this book); the UK of course excludes the Irish Republic, the Channel Islands and the Isle of Man (territories with many unique surnames). A reasonable estimate would be that for the pre-1945 surname stock of the British Isles there is something in the region of 300,000–400,000 surnames. Very many of these have not made it into any surname dictionary.

The biggest problem with the dictionaries concerns accuracy. We have a tendency to believe that if something is published it must be right. However, in the case of the surname dictionaries this is very often not the case. Very many proposed etymologies are simply wrong, and many more need to be treated with caution.

If you really want to know what your surname means you need to do the research yourself.

Surname drift

Surname drift is the process by which unfamiliar sounds are replaced by familiar sounds or even familiar words.

Take for example the surname Horwich, which derives from the village in Lancashire of the same name. For people who lived in the vicinity of Horwich it is reasonable to expect that their surname would be spelt in the same way as the village. However, once families moved away from the locality, spelling more easily changed. For this surname the initial H was the first casualty, leading to Oridge. Now Oridge doesn't seem to mean anything at all, so there is an inbuilt instability in the form. A subsequent modification leads to Orange. This form is easy to pronounce and is likely to be stable, for once a surname is associated with a common noun the drift is in effect stopped.

There is no simple way of getting back from Orange to Horwich. For surnames of this nature it may be that careful genealogical research can unearth the origin. It is however too easy to jump to a false etymology. Suggestions that Orange means a supporter of Prince William of Orange or a nickname for someone with an orange complexion or orange-red hair have both been made for this name, but they are simply fiction. Take whatever you might find in a surname dictionary with a big pinch of salt.

SPELLING

Surname spelling needs to be approached with considerable care. There are several factors which encouraged variant spelling.

- Individuals in past ages did not share our view that a name has only one correct spelling. We have several signatures of William Shakespeare, in which he spells his name in three different ways.

- Literacy was rare at the time of surname formation and for some centuries following. The preserved spellings are therefore those written down by a clerk, who recorded what he thought he heard.

- Formal and informal spellings were often distinguished, so the same name could have two spellings.

- The language changed so that the way a surname was pronounced would change. This might be reflected in the spelling.

Figure 5. Spelling was once fluid, as this autograph of William Shakespeare reminds us – here the bard spells his surname 'Shakspeare'.

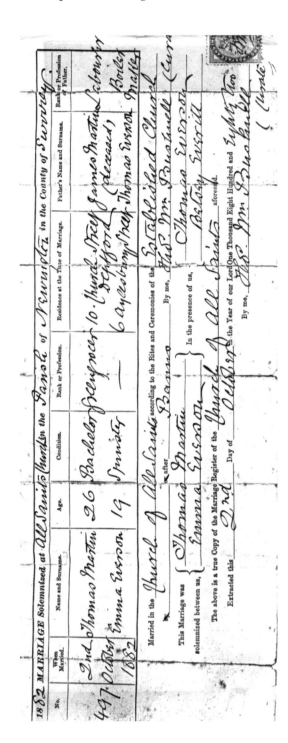

Figure 6. Officials' mistakes are a major source of spelling variants. In this 1882 marriage certificate the bride's surname Everson is also the surname of two of the witnesses, but these are written once as Everson and once as Everitt.

There are also factors which encouraged one spelling to be maintained.

- The minimum level of literacy may be considered to be the ability to write your own name. Often this was little more than drawing a remembered set of symbols, or saying the remembered names of the letters which make up a name. Many people who signed with an X could nonetheless spell their name.

- In families, often someone knew how a name should be spelt and was present on formal occasions.

- Often a local official or minister would know how a name was spelt.

The issue of formal and informal spellings is illustrated by the surname Taylor. This is an occupation name, from tailor, but with the I changed to Y. Early spellings of the name show both forms, but today Taylor, perceived as the more formal spelling, is almost universal. The formality of the spelling Y over I appears to apply only to surnames of two syllables or more (by contrast we have Smith, Hill, King) and only when the I is stressed (so we have unstressed I vowels in Martin, Davis, Harris). It doesn't work where the surname is strongly associated with a first name (as in Phillips) or where the origin is Welsh (as in Price). Indeed, I'm very close to saying that it is a phenomenon specific to the surname Taylor.

The final -e spelling of many surnames also seems to add a sense of formality. Surnames may have a silent -e at the end, as in Clarke and Moore. Clarke once sounded it; Moore never did.

THE SURNAME REVOLUTION

Today we can speak of a revolution in surname studies. The traditional way of studying surnames has been the etymological or philological approach. This has treated surnames as proper nouns whose origins may be investigated in much the same way as any other word in the English language. Just as the *Oxford English Dictionary* works 'on historical principles' by which the earliest forms are noted and an etymology is offered for every word, so scholars studying surnames have sought to do just the same for surnames. This traditional foundation to surname study is indispensable, but it is now supplemented with three new tools which are a true revolution in our understanding.

1. The genealogical approach of tracing lines back to their medieval origins. It is only the recent information revolution, which has made so many genealogical resources easily accessible and searchable, that has truly permitted this approach. We have moved into an age where many hundreds of lines can indeed be traced back to a point of origin.

2. The distribution approach of analysing where a surname occurs. It is the recent advances in databases that have made this truly practical, especially for the more common surnames. There are indeed earlier studies, but what once took many hours of labour can now be accomplished at the touch of a button.

3. The genetic approach. Surely the most exciting development is the mass availability of technology which enables genetic relationships to be established.

Family Names of the United Kingdom, a project from the University of West of England led by Richard Coates, is set to transform our knowledge of United Kingdom surnames. It aims to take significant steps towards reliable explanations of all the current family names and to offer the best achievable account of their geographical and linguistic origins. Results will be available through a database which should offer a synthesis of the best available evidence and interpretation. It will be a super resource – but is not expected before 2014 at the earliest.

Figure 7. The first edition of P. G. Wodehouse's *Psmith in the City*, which aimed to catch its readers' attention by the upwardly mobile spelling of Smith.

Your local library

The surname dictionaries are worth a look. Be warned that the quality is not high. You are unlikely to want to buy them, but they are readily found in libraries. The main ones are:

▶ *British Family Names* (1894) by Henry Barber. This volume has stood the test of time and is a quality source of information.

▶ *A Dictionary of English Surnames* (many editions; most recent is 1997) by P. H. Reaney and R. M. Wilson. This dictionary carries the authority of publisher Oxford University Press and has been extensively marketed – it is in effect the dictionary every English library has on its shelves. In my view it contains more error than truth.

▶ *A Dictionary of Surnames* (1988) by Patrick Hanks and Flavia Hodges. Again published by Oxford University Press. It avoids excessive duplication of Reaney and Wilson by covering the whole of the British Isles and with some coverage of the whole of Europe.

▶ *Family Names and Family History* (2000) by David Hey.

▶ *Dictionary of English and Welsh Surnames* (1901) by C. W. Bardsley.

▶ *The Penguin Dictionary of Surnames* (1994) by Basil Cottle.

▶ *Scottish Surnames* (new edition 2002) by David Dorward. This is probably the best of the surname dictionaries and good news if your interest is in Scottish surnames.

Evaluating sources

We have a predisposition to assume that because it is written in a book it must be right. In fact the majority of printed explanations of surname origin are simply wrong and so littered with basic errors that it is obvious their authors have no academic grounding whatsoever in the subject they are discussing. Even worse are instances of companies that sell such fiction as if it were fact. Anthony Hope (in *Tracing Your Family History*, Collins, 2004) is rightly critical of this practice: 'certificates...are copied straight out of surname dictionaries, usually, it seems, by people with very little understanding of the subject and very low powers of concentration. They mostly contain misleading statements or plain old mistakes'.

Let's examine a typical entry about a surname. The example below is in quality a little better than the average as it does actually include within it some occasional correct information. It is by an anonymous researcher published in a 2003 book and edited by a genealogy magazine – and perhaps it is well that it is anonymous as this saves the author's blushes.

Bates
An English and Scottish surname derived from the pet form of the first name Bartholomew (Middle English Bat(t)e). Bartholomew was a common medieval name – from the Hebrew meaning 'son of Talmai' (abounding in the furrows). Another example of the root is Bateman – who would have been a servant of Bartholomew.

The Bates surname may also derive from the Old English word 'bat' meaning bate. Yet another source originates from the Old Norse word 'bati' which means 'dweller by a fat pasture'.

The description of this surname does contain some correct information:

▶ That Bates is from the late medieval name Bartholomew is almost certainly correct – though the name would usually be described as being from the late medieval period, not from the Middle English language.

▶ That the surname Bateman is in origin a servant of someone called Bates is plausible; a servant of someone called Bartholomew (as suggested) is less likely.

▶ Bartholomew was indeed a common name in past times, from the late Middle Ages until the mid-19th century.

The description contains information which is irrelevant or doubtful.

▶ The derivation of the Christian name Bartholomew is a matter for students of the New Testament and the Aramaic language and has no bearing on the surname.

▶ The surname is an English name. While found in Scotland today, this represents migration from England to Scotland.

▶ Variant spellings of the short form of Bartholomew include Bate, Batte and Bat. These are simply spelling variants. The key point – that 'Bate' is the short form of Bartholomew just as 'Tom' is the short form of Thomas – rather gets lost.

The description contains information which is wrong.

▶ Bartholomew is in fact from the Aramaic language, not the Hebrew language.

▶ 'Talmai' does not mean 'abounding in furrows'. And anyway, what is 'abounding in furrows' supposed to mean? Rather the name means in Aramaic 'son of the farmer'. However, this is not relevant to the surname.

▶ No British Isles surnames come from Old English.

▶ There is an Old English word *bat*. The description says it is from *bate*, surely a typo of *boat*. Yes, Old English *bat* means *boat*. But it doesn't mean boatman or anything comparable.

▶ Almost no British Isles surnames come from Old Norse.

▶ The Old Norse word *bati* does not mean 'dweller by a fat pasture'.

This description is a little better than the average offered by books, magazines and dictionaries. It does at least contain some correct information within it, which actually counts as an achievement. Notwithstanding, it is abysmal, and it is sad that such utter rubbish is routinely presented as if it were academically sound.

ACTIVITY

Spotting likely errors

▶ The surname is from Anglo-Saxon or Old English. Oh no it's not! Not a single British Isles surname can be shown to be from the Anglo-Saxon or Old English period. It might be an old English occupation (with a small o), but that is something completely different.

▶ The surname is from the Vikings or the Old Norse language. There are a handful of surnames in this category, but treat such statements with great caution. In particular, British Isles surnames ending in –son are not Viking, though often claimed to be.

▶ The surname is Norman. Possibly. There are a few surnames in this category, though most surnames claimed to have come across with William the Conqueror and to have been borne by people who fought at the Battle of Hastings are in fact not in this category.

▶ The surname is from Germanic, Latin, Greek or Hebrew. Oh no it's not! Never!

▶ The surname is linked with a legend of origin. Treat with the very greatest suspicion. Most legends were made up centuries after the surname. A very few might just possibly be correct.

▶ The surname is a nickname. Probably not. There are nicknames among British Isles surnames, but the category is not common. You can pretty much discount the absurd ones, of the nature 'Drake is the surname of someone who looked like a duck'. You can also discount ones which apply to a distinguishing characteristic, as in 'Brown is the surname of someone who had brown hair'.

▶ The surname has multiple origins. Some certainly do, but this is nowhere near as common as some writers appear to suggest.

Spotting likely truths

▶ The surname is from a place name, particularly a place which can be identified.

▶ The surname is a trade name.

▶ The surname is a patronymic meaning 'son of' plus first name.

▶ The name was brought to the British Isles by Romany Gypsies or Jews or Huguenots or some other named group. Strictly of course this isn't a surname origin, just a point of arrival in the British Isles.

▶ The surname is strongly localized in one part of the British Isles.

Definitions that look promising might include that Bellingham is from Bellingham (Northumberland), Brewer is from the occupation brewer, Johnson is the son of John, Solomon is a Jewish surname, Sloecombe is a Devonshire name. Of course if any of these surnames happen to be yours (and in many cases even if they are not) you probably know this anyway.

3

Exploring Surname Distribution

A key piece of information about a surname is to know where it is from. An excellent guide to this is its present-day distribution. Surnames tend to stay put over the centuries.

THE HOMES OF ENGLISH FAMILY NAMES

The book which launched the study of surname distribution is Henry Brougham Guppy's *The Homes of English Family Names* (1890). Guppy is still the starting point for examining surname distribution.

Guppy's work reminds us that what we now do with a database could once be done with pen and paper. His study was carried out in the 1880s – at a time when the population was less mobile than today – and restricted to the category of yeoman farmers, which Guppy reasonably assumed were a class relatively stationary from generation to generation because they were tied to inherited lands. His work is restricted to England, though the concepts are applicable elsewhere.

He observed the differing spread of surnames, classifying them in six broad groups:

1. general names (found in most counties);
2. common names (found in 20–29 counties);
3. regional names (found in 10–19 counties);
4. district names (found in 4–9 counties);
5. county names (found in two or three counties – additionally Guppy usually established an origin in just one county);
6. peculiar names (found in one county, or even in just a part of one county).

These categories are still useful. For example, of the 50 most common surnames examined in Appendix 1 of this book, only three fit Guppy's definition of 'general' names (Clark, Cook and Smith). Most of the 50 most common surnames listed in this book are not 'general' but 'common', which means that rather than occurring everywhere they have a regional distribution that Guppy found meaningful. Were Guppy's study to cover the whole of the British Isles (rather than just England) it seems that all surnames save Smith would be 'common' rather than 'general'. Guppy serves to remind us that (almost) all British Isles surnames are to some degree regional.

At the other end of Guppy's spectrum are names that are linked with a single county. Thus for example Guppy identifies Clutterbuck as a Gloucestershire name, and notes a Clowterbuck as Mayor of Gloucester in 1545. In the 1880s nearly half of people with this surname lived in Gloucestershire (and most of the rest in neighbouring counties, particularly Somerset). Even today many people who have this surname will be from the county of Gloucestershire, or be aware of a family origin there. We are probably safe to say that every Clutterbuck has Gloucestershire roots, and every Clutterbuck is related. Sometimes Guppy becomes even more precise. Thus Tucker is certainly a Devonshire name, but Guppy feels able to locate it specifically in Barnstaple. He is probably correct.

DIRECTORIES AND DISTRIBUTION

Until very recently surname distribution was examined with a lot of counting and a lot of calculating. The most common source has been telephone directories.

The process is laborious. For each telephone directory it is necessary to count the number of occurrences of the required name, as well as the total number of names in the directory. This can be expressed as a percentage. The process is repeated with every telephone directory for an area, perhaps the island of Ireland. The results indicate where a surname is most and least common. Much of the process is common sense, but for those interested in the maths there is a specialist book on the topic.[1] The only good reason today for using directories may be if you were in a part of the world where an online source is not available.

NATIONAL TRUST NAMES

National Trust Names at **www.nationaltrustnames.org.uk** is a superb online site for the distribution of surnames in Great Britain (not Northern Ireland or the Republic of Ireland). A few clicks is all it takes to find the distribution of a surname in 1881, and if required, to compare it with its present-day distribution.

Results from the site indicate that dispersion of names follows three basic patterns.

1 Colin D. Rogers (1995) *The Surname Detective: Investigating Surname Distribution in England 1086 – Present Day,* Manchester University Press.

■ A surname is concentrated in one location, and spreads out in all directions from this central point. This is typical of families attached to the land, effectively the yeoman class of England and the tenant farmers of Wales and Ireland – it is not a typical Scottish pattern.

■ A surname is concentrated in one location and spreads in a linear form along a road through migration. Thus a surname might be encountered along a stretch of the Great North Road (today's A1).

■ A surname is concentrated in several distinct locations. This suggests an early dispersal by a number of highly mobile individuals, probably aristocrats.

These three basic dispersal patterns may be blended, so that a particular surname may show elements of two of them.

ACTIVITY

Online sources
For the surnames of Great Britain the online sources are hard to beat. Investigate the surname you are interested in at National Trust Names – **www.nationaltrustnames.org.uk** – in a few clicks you should have a neat map showing you where the surname is most commonly found. A search engine inquiry for 'surname distribution' will produce some additional sites which give Great Britain distribution maps. The results are comparable to those on National Trust Names, but there are differences depending on the source data used and the rationale behind the presentation. There are also sites which cover North America.

ACTIVITY

Paper sources
Surname distribution can be worked out using any directories which give coverage over the required area. Key sources are the following.

▶ Trade directories. These are copious throughout the 19th century and well into the 20th century. Libraries typically hold trade directories for their own area, perhaps a county, but nationwide cover is found only in major national libraries. If your interest is in distribution within a county then trade directories are a good source.

▶ Electoral registers. Electoral registers past and present are held by public libraries. In theory they are a rich source. In practice there are problems in using them. They are ordered by place, not surname, and only a few of the earlier registers have been indexed by amateurs, so the reality for most locations is that electoral registers cannot be used. The law on access to current electoral records is unclear and subject to local interpretation, with some libraries applying restrictions also to old electoral registers. Most libraries now restrict access and in particular restrict copying. You would be unlikely to be allowed to photocopy a page of a modern electoral register and in most libraries librarians have been instructed to be vigilant in prohibiting manual copying. If you need to use electoral registers you may be advised to discuss access and copying with the librarian.

▶ Telephone directories. These are readily available in UK public libraries and provide a source for surname distribution. The complete set of *The Phone Book* runs to around 170 volumes (depending on the exact date) with a great range of lengths – around 200 pages to around 1,000 pages. Wales has 8 volumes and Scotland has 14 volumes, more manageable numbers. About a third of each directory is devoted to residential customers. The arithmetic is reasonably straightforward:

- Start with the number of residential customers on an average page.
- Calculate the number of residential customers in the directory.
- Count the number of the surname you are interested in.
- Work out the percentage of entries which are the surname in question.
- Assign the value of 100 to the area where the surname is most common. For all other areas calculate the relative occurrence of the surname expressed as a percentage of the area in which it is most common.
- Draw up a table or map showing the percentage found in each directory area.

This process is straightforward, but very time-consuming. It is certainly possible, but you would need a very good reason to do it. It is most likely to be of use not for Great Britain but for countries where other sources are not available. Thus South Africa, Australia and New Zealand could reasonably be approached in such a manner.

ACTIVITY

Northern Ireland distributions

Northern Ireland is not covered by National Trust Names or similar online databases. It is covered by just four telephone directories – for Belfast, and for three zones of Northern Ireland, effectively north, central and south. An examination of these four directories is a manageable task. Additionally they do encapsulate the division between the city of Belfast and rural Northern Ireland, as well as dividing the rural areas in a way which appears relevant for the study of surname distribution.

4

One Source or Many?

Some surnames arose just once. There was a single man who was the first bearer of the name. In such circumstances it is likely that all who bear the name are related. Other surnames arose separately more than once. A few have very many points of origin.

MONOGENESIS AND POLYGENESIS

A surname that was formed just once is termed monogenetic. Those formed more than once are polygenetic. Classifying a surname as monogenetic or polygenetic is a key to understanding the name.

There is no agreed method to determine whether a name is monogenetic or polygenetic. The frequency with which a surname occurs is a rule-of-thumb guide, but it must be stressed that not enough research has so far been carried out to know quite where the line should be drawn. Additionally a quantitative approach can only ever be a rough-and-ready indication, and it is far from clear that there is a simple line to be drawn. Yet a benchmark is offered by the name Sykes, which is now accepted as being monogenetic, meaning that there was one original Mr Sykes from whom all subsequent Sykes are descended. Today this surname has around 10,000 bearers in the British Isles alone. Far more study is needed – we need to be acutely aware of the paucity of data so far available – but as a working hypothesis it may be suggested that as Sykes is monogenetic then names less common than Sykes are also likely to be monogenetic.

So how common is Sykes? The most readily available figures are for Great Britain on the basis of the 1881 census, and place the name in 283rd place. As a rule-of-thumb any surname which is less common than Sykes is likely to be monogenetic.

Of the names which are more common than Sykes, some have clearly arisen independently very many times. Smith and Jones, the two most common surnames in the British Isles, are clear examples of polygenesis. Yet somewhere between position 1 (Smith) and position 283 (Sykes) there should be a surname which is the most common name to have arisen by monogenesis. Not enough surnames have been investigated to say much more than this. Of the 50 most common surnames in England (examined in Appendix 1) almost all are surely polygenetic. However, it is just about within the bounds of possibility that Shaw (46), Bennett (48) and Carter (49) will in time come to be shown as monogenetic.

BI-GENESIS AND TRI-GENESIS

There are also cases where names may have arisen just two or three times, which should perhaps be called bi-genesis and tri-genesis categories. There are surnames which have larger (but still finite and precisely known) points of origin. Sometimes we can untangle these surnames.

The surname Cree has been shown to have five origins in the British Isles.

- A Derbyshire and Nottinghamshire family traces to a progenitor born in 1644, where Cree is a shortened form of MacKree, presumably an ancestor from another part of the British Isles who moved to the location.

- Scottish families called Cree trace to a progenitor who is a mid-15th century Perth merchant; the surname appears to be from the place name Crieff.

- A Kent Cree family traces to a Huguenot progenitor, Pierre Jacob Carré.

- The Irish surname Creagh may on occasions be spelt Cree.

- In the Victorian period there is adoption of Cree for foundling children in the City of London parish of St Katherine Creechurch, with more than a dozen individuals given the name – and potentially therefore half a dozen male progenitors.

This rather unusual name therefore traces to four early progenitors and several additional Victorian progenitors from the parish of St Katherine Creechurch. A name which at first sight appears a good candidate for monogenesis in fact has several points of origin. What is remarkable is that work by enthusiasts has enabled these progenitors to be identified.

There are cases when names arose a handful of times. Green, which is the 18th most common name in England and Wales, may plausibly have as few as half a dozen origins, a number small enough to hope that in the future the precise origin of each may be identified.

THE MONOGENETIC REVOLUTION?

Where once it was thought that polygenesis was extremely common, now there is evidence that monogenesis was the normal situation. The big exceptions are Welsh patronymics (discussed below) and a handful of occupation names. But the general trend is that most surnames in the British Isles arose just once. This is certainly the normal state of affairs for unusual ones but it seems to me that even for many of the more common surnames a single origin or a small number of points of origin are likely. This is quite a sea change in thinking about British Isles surnames and may be a monogenetic revolution.

FOUNDLINGS

There are special cases around the surnames of foundlings. In the British Isles foundling babies were often named after the parish which looked after them, or the saint to whom the parish church was dedicated, or sometimes after the precise location in which they were found. Surnames such as Deptford, Mary and Porch may be from such sources. Also used for foundlings was the surname Found. Children who were fostered might be called Foster – though this surname is also an occupational name from a forester.

It is often possible to trace a line back to an 18th or 19th century foundling. While this circumstance is likely to prevent further genealogical progress, it may well produce a unique surname of recent origin, possibly a monogenetic surname.

ACTIVITY

How common is your surname?
This key piece of information is crucial to understanding your surname.

▷ Usually it is straightforward to find a surname frequency from online sources. For example, British Surnames at **www.british surnames.co.uk** is an excellent source. There are plenty of others. Inevitably what is available online changes rapidly, but a search engine will find sources for 'British surname frequencies'. They all give slightly different answers (depending on the data they have used) but they (mostly) give similar answers.

▷ Beware that a database may cover Great Britain, or just England and Wales. The whole UK or the whole of the British Isles do not appear to be covered by any one database.

▷ Irish surnames and those of the Channel Islands and Isle of Man are special cases. There are some ideas within the appropriate chapters in this book.

5

Working with Occupational Names

One of the biggest groups of surnames is of those derived from occupations. Many of them are very easy to spot: Baker, Brewer, Smith, Clerk, Weaver, Mason and Taylor. The convention of an occupation being passed from father to son facilitated the adoption of occupation names as surnames. Names of this sort are more common in England than elsewhere in the British Isles.

THE AGE OF OCCUPATIONAL NAMES

Most British Isles occupational names started in the 13th and 14th centuries. There are certainly earlier and later examples, but an age of around six or seven centuries – maybe up to two dozen generations – is a good starting assumption for these surnames.

The occupations remembered are of course those of a past age. Some of them may not be immediately obvious today because the occupation name has changed or the occupation has been lost. Thus Fletcher is the surname of an arrow maker while Furrier is someone who worked with animal pelts.

UNIQUE OCCUPATIONAL NAMES

The more common occupational names are presumably poly-

Figure 8. Sir Henry Cooper made his name as a heavyweight boxing champion. His surname suggests a cooper or barrel-maker, and in this photograph he combines boxing gloves with tools more appropriate to his surname.

genetic, that is, created many times. Future study may well identify a handful of originators of widespread surnames such as Brewer and Baker – or may alternatively conclude that there were very many occasions when these surnames were adopted. Unusual occupational names are likely to be monogenetic. Thus for example Shakespeare (a pike-man in the medieval army) is probably an example of an occupational name with a single point of origin.

STATUS NAMES

A special subgroup of occupation names is status names reflecting an office held, such as Marshall, Chamberlaine and Reeve (from shire-reeve or sheriff). Hunt falls into this category as a name for a huntsman, someone who looked after the stags and boars, usually for the king. The two first records of the name are both early in the 13th century. Humphrey le Hunte is found in Sussex in 1203 (Feet of Fines) while a few years later in 1219 Ralph Hunt is found in Yorkshire (Yorkshire assizes). Possibly these men are related, but the geographical distance suggests that the name may have arisen two or more times.

ACTIVITY

The occupations of past ages

▶ The *Oxford English Dictionary* is the definitive resource for the names of occupations. The full-length version of this dictionary (a subscription database available free in UK public libraries) gives a definition along with the date first recorded, subsequent examples of its use, variant spellings and an etymology.

▶ Dialect dictionaries give regional occupations. Most English and Welsh counties have a late-Victorian dialect dictionary and frequently later county volumes – libraries keep the volumes for their region. Scotland has national coverage (again a subscription database available for free through public libraries).

▶ Online there are certainly descriptions of medieval occupations. Beware – many seem somewhat fanciful.

6

Focusing on Place Names

At its simplest a surname and a place name will be identical, and the surname will derive from the place name. Sometimes it really is that simple.

Figure 9. Many English place names have given rise to surnames, including most (perhaps all) of the place names on this West Sussex signpost.

COMPLICATIONS OF PLACE-NAME SURNAMES

There are, however, all sorts of complicating factors.

- Place names have themselves changed over the centuries. For example, the Domesday Book (1086) forms of place names are frequently different from the forms we know today. Even in the 13th and 14th centuries, when most surnames came into being, place names had often not assumed their present forms.

- Many place names have vanished, often as the settlement they refer to has itself vanished.

- Many surnames derive from very small communities or from names for areas of land, which are often not well recorded in modern atlases.

- Many places have nicknames as well as official names – and often it is the nicknames that give rise to surnames. London's Petticoat Lane is famous worldwide yet it appears on the map under its official name of Middlesex Street.

- Places can take their names from people. It is much more likely that a farmhouse will take its name from a person than vice versa.

The strongest ground for someone being named after a place is that they actually own that place. The practice is still found in Scotland where the owner of a particular estate is usually called Laird of that estate, with the title passing with the property. In England the equivalent is Lord of the Manor, with the courtesy title of Lord. Again the title passes with the estate, and today it is even possible to purchase fragments of land which were once part of a big estate and to which the legal title Lord of the Manor is attached. Such lordships can in effect be bought and sold.

In medieval usage estate titles were used much as we use surnames. The lands were passed from father to son, so the estate title was transmitted much as a surname is. Additionally the son of a landowner was frequently granted the title Master plus the name of the estate. In such circumstances it was easy for an estate name to convert to a surname.

As a starting point it is most probable that someone who bears a place-name surname is descended from the owner of that estate.

MIGRATION AND PLACE-NAME SURNAMES

It is also possible for someone who has a place-name surname to acquire it simply by coming from that place. However, the usage only makes sense if the person moves away so that in the vicinity where they are living the place name is sufficiently unusual to be a useful descriptor. And once people had moved away from a location where everyone knew the place name, there is more chance of corruption of the original place name, and of the surname formed. Thus for example the name of the English town of Grantham was taken to Scotland by one of the followers of King David of Scotland, who first appears in Scotland as William de Graham. Subsequently the surname appears as Graham. The surname is today associated with Scotland, made famous by the family of the Dukes of Montrose whose family name it was and by John Graham, the Jacobite hero remembered as Bonny Dundee. Yet the surname moved again – from Scotland to Cumberland, reflecting the cross-border interests of the Graham family – and is statistically more common in the English county of Cumberland than it is in Scotland.

Spelling can be inventive. For example, the surname Tortoiseshell is from Tattershall (Lincolnshire); Deadham is from Debenham (Suffolk).

Some surnames identify an individual as being from a nation. Leading examples include Britton (from Brittany), Fleming (from Flanders), Pettingale (from Portugal) and France. Similarly, county surnames are found in families that moved away from that county. Many British Isles counties have become surnames, with Wiltshire and Worcester/Wooster clear examples.

ODDITIES OF PLACE-NAME SURNAMES

William Camden (writing in 1605) identified a curious set of place-name surnames deriving from inn signs, and which may be borne by the family of the innkeeper. Camden asserts that Dolphin, Bull, Racket and Peacock are all from this source, so these curious surnames are in fact place names, but that very special sort of place name that is the name of an inn. It is noteworthy that an early form of the surname Bell is shown in the form *John atte Belle*, *John at the Bell*. This name too may be from an inn name.

As well as place names creating surnames, so surnames can create place names. Thus a village can be named after a family, as Stoke Mandeville (Buckinghamshire) after the Mandeville family. Countless farmhouses and fields are named from owners, and as towns and cities expanded it became customary to name streets after the landowners who owned the site, or the developer who built on it, or to commemorate a famous person, often with a local association. One of the most extreme examples is a group of streets in London to the south of the Strand:

- George Court;
- Villiers Street;
- Duke Street (now demolished);
- Of Alley (now renamed York Place);
- Buckingham Street.

These five streets remember the former owner of the land on which they stand: George Villiers, Duke of Buckingham.

For those seeking the origin of surnames such cases can be confusing. It could seem plausible that the Mandeville family took their name from the village of Stoke Mandeville, and their connection with the village is indeed strong. However, the village is named after the family, not vice versa.

ACTIVITY

The road atlas
▶ Simply looking in the index of a road atlas may give an idea of whether a surname might plausibly be from a place name.
▶ Place-name glossaries (including those available online) give information about smaller places.
▶ A trip to a library will give access to national and county-by-county place-name dictionaries which seek to give the etymology of place names. A surname develops from the form of a place name at the time when the surname first appeared.

ACTIVITY

Visiting the place
If you can identify a place which gives rise to the surname you are researching, you might like to make a visit there.
▶ If the name is linked with the Lord of the Manor there may well be

manorial records in a library or record office. A local studies library or county record office are the places to start.

▶ The parish church may contain monuments and inscriptions dating back to the time of surname formation, perhaps including early forms of the name.

▶ Local history groups are likely to be interested in local surnames.

▶ Beware! Often place-name surnames are only meaningful when a person moves away from a place, so the link between a surname you are interested in and a place may well be tenuous.

7

Making Sense of Landscape Names

Landscape names – sometimes called topographic names – are one of the major sources of UK surnames. Arguably they are best regarded as a subset within place names, but there is a long tradition of treating them separately.

THE THEORY

The basic idea is that people may have been identified by reference to a landscape feature, perhaps because they owned it or simply because they lived near it. It is usually considered that there are three common types.

1. The simple name of the landscape feature, such as Hill, Cliff, River. Sometimes a patronymic ending is added as in Rivers, the son of Mr River. Spellings may be modified, so Cliff becomes Clift.

2. The form preposition plus landscape feature, as in Atwater and Underhill.

3. The form landscape feature +er, as in Downer, a Sussex name reflecting the regional descriptive name 'down' for a chalk hill.

THE PRACTICE

The category is very hard to interpret. First of all it is not clear that all surnames that appear to be simply landscape names really are members of this category. The surname Hill looks like a simple reference to someone who lived on a hill. But it could also be someone who lived in or owned a place called Hill, as there are villages by this name in Gloucestershire and Warwickshire. The surname might also be a reduced form of a place name which contains the element 'hill', and Hill is therefore a place-name surname.

There are also names frequently asserted to be landscape names, but whose derivation is frankly suspect. Thus Noakes and Nash are supposedly landscape names from the phrases *atten oakes* and *atten ashe*, meaning 'at the oak trees' and 'at the ash tree'. Well maybe, and certainly this derivation for these names has been repeated by countless surname books establishing a degree of authority by frequent reiteration. Yet it is problematic both on linguistic grounds and on rational grounds. Linguistically the preposition *at* in Middle English is in fact *atte*, not *atten*. It is true that an –n– sound could be inserted to make it flow off the tongue, but there is no real need for this. Additionally it is not clear why the preposition used should be *at* and not *by*, nor why the (redundant) –n– has been retained. Rationally describing some-one as living at oak trees or at an ash tree seems weak. In my view there is an argument for considering Noakes and Nash as landscape names, but there is also an argument for saying they are probably something else.

The practice of dealing with landscape names is therefore to treat all of them with suspicion. Very often surnames that look like a landscape name are in fact something else. Take for example the surname Holmes, which if it is a landscape name means someone who lived by a holm oak, an etymology proposed in very many surname dictionaries. Yet this is not likely. It more probably relates to *holm*, a now obsolete word for an island in a bay or river and a frequent place-name element. Holmes may well be a shortened form of a specific place name including the element 'holm'.

ACTIVITY

Landscape names

▶ If you think you are dealing with a landscape name, stop and think again.

▶ Could it be a true place name, perhaps a reduced form?

▶ Could it be an occupational name, perhaps based on an occupation with which we are no longer familiar?

▶ Could it be something else?

The result should be that you pause before classifying any surname as a landscape name. Ideas within this book may indicate a way of finding the origin.

8

Working with Patronymics

In English a patronymic is usually a reduced form of a noun phrase in the form *Thomas, William's son.* The form may be reduced either to *Thomas Williams* (in effect including the *'s* of the genitive ending and leaving off the son element as superfluous) or to *Thomas Williamson* (with the *son* element included and the *'s* dropped as superfluous). The basic structure of the phrase is unchanged from Anglo-Saxon to Modern English. In the 13th century (when many sur-names were formed) it would be spelt as *Thomas, Williames sunu.*

Figure 10. The sons of Peter, Magnus, John and Eirik feature on these four Icelandic stamps. Iceland is the one European nation which routinely uses patronymics rather than surnames.

WILLIAM, WILLIAMS OR WILLIAMSON?

Quite why the form used is sometimes *William*, sometimes *Williams* and sometimes *Williamson* has not received a consistent answer from surname specialists. It has long been noted that within England, patronymics in the form –*s* are more often encountered in the South and West, while those in the form –*son* are characteristic of the North and East (and to some extent to Lowland Scotland). It has been observed that the division is on the line of the old Danelaw, with the counties of England to the North and East being those that absorbed most Danish Viking migrants, while the counties of the South and West are those that most successfully resisted. It has been just a step from this observation to note that the patronymic –*son* is indeed a form used by the Danish Vikings in their Old Norse language, and to assert that surnames in –*son* are Viking. Countless books on names repeat this story.

Yet surnames in England post-date the Viking invasion by some centuries. This oft-repeated explanation cannot possibly be correct – at least not in the simple way it is stated.

The English patronymic form has much to do with the date. In broad brush terms there are three types of patronymics, and three centuries of formation.

12th century	name alone	**William**
13th century	name with –*s*	**Williams**
14th century	name with –*son*	**Williamson**

As surnames were formed first in the south of England and surname formation spread north and west through the British Isles we can see that the name alone is a feature of the extreme south (for example, it is found in Sussex), that the form in *–s* is found in much of the South and Midlands, and that the form in *–son* is characteristic of the North, Scotland and Ireland. The patronymic form has more to do with date of formation than anything else. What we are seeing is evidence that surname formation occurred in different places at different dates.

Notwithstanding, the mistaken association of *–son* forms with the Vikings probably contains at least a grain of truth. A consequence of the Danish Viking migration to England was changes in the regional dialects of English – changes which even today can be noted between the northern and southern dialects of English, where those of the north still bear witness to the impact of the Vikings. In the English south and west of the Danelaw, the standard form was *Thomas, Williames sunu*. Here the genitive ending of William is *–es*, which is more than just a strange spelling as it really was pronounced 'es'. Additionally the word for *son* was not *sun* but *sunu*, with two syllables clearly pronounced. The logical way to shorten *Thomas Williames sunu* was simply *Thomas Williames*, and as in time the ending became reduced the name became *Thomas Williams*. But north and east of the Danelaw line the impact of the Vikings' Old Norse language was a genitive singular that was merely a sibilant (an 's' sound), plus a shortening of *sunu* to *sun* or *son*. The form is therefore *Thomas Williams son* which readily became *Thomas Williamson*.

FORGOTTEN FIRST NAMES

A curious category is patronymics deriving from first names which are no longer used. Very many of these are what are sometimes regarded as Anglo-Saxon first names, which has led countless name books and online sites into the error of arguing that a name is Anglo-Saxon in origin. While the rule by Anglo-Saxon kings ended in 1066, neither the language nor the culture of the Anglo-Saxons ended then. Most people continued to speak a form of the Anglo-Saxon language and continued to use Anglo-Saxon first names, and this naming practice continued at least until the end of the 13th century, by which time English had developed into Middle English. And even in the later Middle English period some Anglo-Saxon first names continued – while at various later dates these Anglo-Saxon names have been revived.

From among the mass of Anglo-Saxon first names which continued in use well after the Norman Conquest are many that gave rise to surnames. Allwright is plausibly from Aethelric (and an early patronymic which is just the bare name, without –s or – son), and similarly Darwin is from Deorwine. It needs to be stressed that these are not Anglo-Saxon surnames; rather they are late medieval surnames formed on the basis of Anglo-Saxon first names which happened to survive the demise of Anglo-Saxon England.

Nicknames were also a source of patronymics, and many of these nicknames are not common today. Dogge and Dod as nicknames for Roger are not usual today – though many will be familiar with *The Beano* comic character 'Roger the Dodger' or Charles Dickens' 'Artful Dodger' in *Oliver Twist*. These nicknames have given rise to Dodgson. Similarly Daw for Ralph is not familiar today, though it gives rise to Dawson and Dawkins.

Many names from first names are not immediately obvious. Some examples include the following.

Ball	Baldwin
Cole	Nicholas
Elliot	Elias
Gibbons	Gilbert
Gilham	William
Hamley	Hamo
Hancock	John
Hudson	Huck
Kitt	Christopher
Maykin	Matthew
Ransome	Randal
Saunders	Alexander
Tamblin	Thomas
Tennyson	Denis

KINSHIP NAMES

As well as straightforward patronymics, there are names which express kinship with a named person. Typically these are names which end in *–kin*, *–cock* or *–cox*, surnames such as Malkyn, Adcock and Wilcox. These mean the kin or family of a particular name.

Very occasionally more distant relationships can be expressed in surnames. The ending *–magh* meaning brother-in-law is found in Hickmott and Watmough.

METRONYMS

Surnames based on a woman's name are far less common than

those of a man, but they certainly exist. The technical name for these is metronyms. They are probably from women who were heiresses, or who were widowed early, thereby gaining effective control of their husbands' estates. Often the relationship may be less direct than a child, rather we should see the name as meaning kin of the woman described. Malkyn appears to be the kin of Maud; the woman in this case may be the Empress Maud. Catt and Catling are kin of Catherine or Kate; Marguerite the kin of Margaret; Dyott is kin of Dye, a nickname for Denise; Cash is kin of Cassandra. Endings in –s or –son are unusual though they are found. Annison is son of Agnes (not Ann), Edison son of Edith and Maddison son of Magdalene.

THE PROCESS IN REVERSE

Take care – it is possible for the process to go the other way, and for a surname to give rise to a first name. This is particularly common in the case of Scottish surnames, where surnames such as Douglas, Gordon and Graham have produced identical first names.

BACK TO A POINT OF ORIGIN

Patronymics are not the most promising names to take back to an original founder, the man with the first name alone. But it can be done. One such name is Adair. The starting point with this name is to strip away the myth. It has long been interpreted in terms of a folk etymology – that the name derives from a wayward son of Earl Desmond of Adair (in Ireland) who settled in Scotland – but this story must be completely rejected, for the name is found in Scotland well before the age of Earl Desmond. The earliest bearer of the surname is Thomas Edzear or Odeir, who in the early 14th century received lands on the Rhins of Galloway from King Robert the Bruce. The variant spellings – Edzear and Odeir/Adair – persist until at least the early 17th century, before settling in the present form Adair. The –z– of Edzear is a Scottish spelling convention for –g–, the name being pronounced 'Edgear' and meaning 'Edgar's son'. It is therefore a patronymic. In this case the original Edgar can be identified, as one of the leaders of the Battle of the Standard. This Edgar is son of Duvenald, son of Donegal of Morton Castle.

ACTIVITY

Is it a patronymic?
- If it ends in –s or –son, yes it probably is.
- In these cases you should be able to identify the first name. First-name dictionaries (both in libraries and online) list first names with which you may be unfamiliar. Bible dictionaries list Bible names, many of which have been used as first names in the British Isles.
- Nicknames are frequently more challenging as they are less well recorded and often not intuitive. Many nicknames are from the second syllable of personal names, such as Bert from Robert. Reflection might suggest a likely first name.
- Names without a final –s or –son may be patronymics, but consider other possibilities set out in this book.
- Patronymics from outside of England show different formation. Within this book see in particular the chapters on Wales, Scotland, Ireland and the Isle of Man.

9

Taking Care with Nicknames

Nicknames are established in the literature of surname studies and in surname dictionaries as a major source of surnames both in the British Isles and internationally. Alexander Pope (in his translation of Homer's *The Iliad*) tells us that 'The epithets of great men...were in the nature of surnames, and repeated as such.' Homer himself speaks of 'far-darting Phoebus', the 'blue-eyed Pallas', the 'swift-footed Achilles' and such epithets are at the stage before the formation and potential sources of surnames. Pope goes on to quote Hesiod, who saw such epithets as appropriate both to the gods of Olympus and to the heroes of the Trojan war. Clearly nicknames can become epithets and it should be no surprise that epithets can become surnames.

DISTRUSTING NICKNAMES

Nicknames is an area which needs to be treated with suspicion. When you see in a surname dictionary or an online resource that a surname is a nickname, you should treat this with the greatest of care. While this origin may just possibly be right, more likely than not it is wrong. Therefore look hard for another origin.

Academic scepticism to nicknames as a frequent origin for surnames is strong, and was well established during the first half of the 20th century. Such origins are rare whether considering the British Isles as a whole, or any of the parts of the British Isles:

> Everything goes to show that we must be very cautious in accepting the face signification of a name that looks and sounds as a nickname.
>
> Rev. S. Baring-Gould (1913) *Family Names and Their Story*

> [On nicknames] '...this source is very rare...'
>
> Joseph Storer Clouston (1924) The Peoples and Surnames of Orkney, *Orkney Antiquarian Society Proceedings, v2*

> What on superficial examination appear to have been personal epithets are often something entirely different, misunderstandings arising through failure to grasp various processes of corruption, modification or mutation...There is no necessity whatsoever to suppose that nicknames have originated any of the modern British surnames...having once become obsessed with the idea that surnames are derived from vulgar epithets, discovery of origin becomes easy.
>
> C. L'Estrange Ewen (1931) *A History of Surnames of the British Isles*

> Contrary to the common view I have found few of our surnames to be derived from nicknames.
>
> George F. Black (1946) *The Surnames of Scotland*

These are the lessons of solid scholarship, yet they seem to have been lost in more recent years in the rush towards popular etymologies and the willingness to apply what are often little better than comic supposed origins. In almost all cases the derivations of British Isles surnames from nicknames are simply wrong and any book or online source that routinely suggests such derivations should be treated with the greatest caution, both for these fictitious derivations and perhaps by extension for all derivations the source gives.

Who is to blame?

The biggest single culprit in the popularisation of fake nickname origins appears to be the *Oxford Dictionary of English Surnames*, first published in 1958 and with numerous reprints subsequently. Author P. H. Reaney succumbs to the pressure of a dictionary which feels obliged to offer a definition for all surnames to include nicknames as a claimed etymology for many, then defends this decision with the circular reasoning 'That many modern surnames were originally nicknames is proved conclusively by the material in the following pages'. Reaney would have us believe that Lamb was first used by someone who was meek, Bull by someone headstrong, Colt by someone frisky – and even Ramshead by someone with a head like a ram and Sheepshanks by someone with legs like a sheep. These fanciful definitions should be given no credence, yet the implied authority of publisher Oxford University Press has caused these and thousands of other false derivations from nicknames to enter countless books on surnames.

Black necked, golden bearded, sickle-footed heavy drinkers

Almost every writer has fallen into this error. Thus for example in *The Surnames of Sussex* (1988), Richard McKinley provides some tidy lists of what he thinks are Sussex surnames based on nicknames of individuals who had the characteristics of the animals named. So under mammals we have Bat, Beaver, Bull, Catt, Cony, Hart, Hogg, Leppard, Otter, Steer; under birds Bullfinch, Crane, Crowe, Dunnock, Fesant, Finch, Nightingale, Peacock, Puttock, Sparrow, Swan, Thrush; under fish Herring, Gurnard, Pilchard and Mackerell. Drinkwater is seen as ironical (for a heavy drinker) while names such as Blackneck, Goldeberde and Sickelfoot are seen as descriptive nicknames, leading to a view of medieval Sussex populated by black-necked, golden-bearded, sickle-footed heavy drinkers. I doubt a single one of this collection of Sussex surnames is truly a nickname.

Some supposed nickname origins have been repeated so often that it becomes hard to challenge them. Campbell is supposedly from Gaelic *caimbeul*, meaning crooked mouth, an etymology found in hundreds of printed sources and countless online sources. It is almost certainly wrong. The difficulty of course is that in criticizing an established view it seems required to offer an alternative origin. The problematic but true answer with this and thousands of other supposed nicknames is that we do not know the origin. We do have early use of the name – the first occurrence being Gilascoppe Cambell on a charter of 1263. The suggestion that Campbell is from *Campo Bello* (battlefield, therefore a place-name origin) seems a fanciful folk etymology though it has encouraged the spelling of the surname with a *p*. That it is a reduced form of MacCathmhaoil (son of the battle chieftain) may have merits – this is certainly a patronymic form of the sort favoured by the Celtic languages. Scotland abounds with such fake etymologies. In a similar vein Cameron supposedly means 'crooked nose', again a fanciful etymology. I cannot advance a derivation for Cameron, but I can be sure that Cameron is most unlikely to be from the source suggested.

Investigating Beard

The issue of supposed nicknames may be explored with the surname Beard. It is generally asserted that the surname Beard is from a nickname describing a man who had a notable beard. Examples can indeed be found of men in the Middle Ages who are described in a text as having a beard – for example, Reaney quotes a 12th century reference to *Aelfsige mid tham berde* – 'the bearded Aelfsige' – but this is just a description, not even a nickname, and certainly not a surname. Indeed if we stop and think about this proposed origin for Beard it is apparent that it is unlikely on many levels. In an age before safety razors most men shaved infrequently – if at all – and there were many men who had beards. Curiously some of the surname dictionaries have been sufficiently conscious of this problem to go out of their way to state that men were in fact almost uniformly clean-shaven in the late Middle Ages, an assertion hard to support. Rather the reality is that many men had some form of beard. Now I suppose it is possible that someone who has a truly outstanding beard might be called in his lifetime, say, 'John the beard', but even this is straining credulity. Then there is the bigger problem of transmission to the next generation. A nickname belongs uniquely to the father and is unlikely to be suitable for a son, and again unlikely to be suitable for a grandson. Then there is the problem that most surnames were in origin selected by their bearers. A man with a noteworthy beard might accept in good spirit the nickname 'John the beard' applied by his friends, but would not state this as his name for official recording.

So where does the surname Beard come from? The idea that it is a straightforward nickname for someone with a beard is so remote that it should probably be ruled out entirely. It could be from the first name Bart, a short form of Bartholomew (a first name and nickname not often encountered today but once much more common) with a straightforward change of –t– to –d–. Beardson and Beards are therefore regular patronymics, meaning Bartholomew's son, and Beard an unremarkable reduced form. Or it may be from a place name: Beard in Derbyshire, or many other place names containing an element resembling 'beard'. Or it could be an English variant spelling of the Scottish surname Baird, of which the National Archives' *Documents Online* gives several examples. It is likely that there are multiple origins for the surname Beard and that few or none of them are nicknames.

More problem nicknames

Similarly, Quick is usually considered to be a nickname for someone who is quick. The surname's home is the South West of England, particularly Devonshire. A village now part of Exeter is Cowick, a plausible place name source for this name – and a far more likely etymology than the adjective 'quick'.

The folly of nicknames as an etymology is well illustrated by Nightingale. It has been asserted that this is a nickname, presumably for someone who has a voice like a nightingale. The surname is distinctive of the North West of England, with a strong localization around Bolton. While Bolton may reasonably have as many good singers as any other location, it lacks nightingales. Quite simply the range of the nightingale does not extend this far north. If we were to argue that Nightingale is from the bird we would have to explain why the name appears in the area where the nightingale does not.

EXPLAINING NICKNAMES

What we are seeing in most of the supposed nickname surnames is a corruption of a name, where a name which once meant something has been replaced by a word in English. From the point of view of surname origins this is frustrating because there is no easy way or regular process whereby we might work backwards from a form of a surname we have to its origin. I am sure that Reaney's idea that Sheepshanks was a surname given to someone with legs like a sheep is simply wrong – but I cannot give a definite alternative etymology to explain the name. For the writer of a surname dictionary the options for this and thousands of other names is either to repeat the error of a nickname origin or to confess ignorance. It seems that most take the former course. Yet once the fanciful definition for Sheepshanks has been rejected we can hope to make some genuine progress in exploring the true meaning of this surname.

WHEN NICKNAMES ARE GENUINE

There are a few instances of the one-off recording of what seem to be nicknames. From Newburgh in Fife we have a 1279 reference to a John Unkutherman ('uncouth man'), a form which should probably be regarded as a malicious recording by a clerk. George Swynhouse ('pig house') turns up in Over Blainslie in 1575, again as a one-off usage. These nicknames were never truly surnames and were recorded only by chance.

So are any surnames plausibly nicknames? Perhaps a few really are. Surnames of this type occur when the nickname is borne by a whole family as if a badge of honour. The outstanding example is Palmer and its variants Palmar and Paumier. In the late Middle Ages a journey to Jerusalem was the ultimate pilgrimage, with the return trip taking a year at least (and frequently longer) and fraught with dangers. Those who made the trip were in the habit of returning with palm, often worn as a cross on their coat or carrying a fragment in a locket. These pilgrims were called 'palmers', and palmer and pilgrim became more or less synonyms in English. The achievement was such that a whole family would wish to identify themselves as the descendants of a Jerusalem pilgrim, and the nickname palmer became a surname. The name is first recorded in the late 12th century with three men in three parts of the country. There is a Sagar Palmer in Devonshire (1176), a Wiger le Palmer in Lincolnshire (1191) and a Richard le Paumere in Middlesex (1198). Potentially this is tri-genesis, though a pilgrimage to Jerusalem could easily have taken place a generation or two before these three men, and just as someone making a journey from England to the Holy Land was certainly mobile, so it is reasonable to assume mobility in his immediate descendants. It may well be that Palmer is an example of an early monogenesis.

Comparable with Palmer are Cockell, Cock and Cockle, names adopted by pilgrims to the shrine of Santiago de Compostela who returned wearing a cockle-shell badge as a memento of this shrine of St James.

Pullrose and Pluckrose – both surnames of Sussex – are surely nicknames. A peculiarity of some land tenement in the late Middle Ages is that it was held on the basis of a peppercorn rent usually expressed in terms of a rent of a rose a year – quite literally the payment to the freeholder of one cut flower. As the tenement rights were inherited so the nickname passed down a family, and these two variants were well placed to become surnames.

Maybe nicknames *could* be based on looks

Russell may plausibly be a nickname from red, meaning red-haired. The Norman French terms are *rous* and *rufus*, and a red-haired man may have borne one of these nicknames almost as a first name. The process of children taking the name as a surname is analogous to that of a patronymic. The name is likely to have arisen twice. It is well represented in the South East of England, particularly Kent, while in Scotland it is centred in Lanarkshire. Reid is more problematic. The name cannot (as some have argued) be taken back to a Kentish 'Leofwine se reade' of around 1016 – the description 'the red' is simply his personal nickname. Similarly the Devonshire 'Aluric thane reda' (early 12th century) is simply a man with a nickname. The surname Reid appears to have arisen in Scotland and is plausibly from the adjective 'red', plausibly from another origin altogether.

LANGUAGE NICKNAMES

There is a group of nickname surnames which describe the language people spoke. A speaker of Scots Gaelic could be called Scott. Similarly a Welsh speaker could be called Welsh, or its variants Walsh and Welch. A Brythonic Celtic language – effectively Welsh – was also spoken in Scotland's Strathclyde region, and has given rise to the Scottish surname Wallace. The Cornish language yields Cornish and Curnow – the latter apparently from the Cornish name for Cornish, Kernewek. In all cases the formation of the names suggests that speaking the languages concerned was remarkable in the areas where they were formed. Thus Welsh is effectively an English name for a Welsh-speaker living in England. Wallace testifies to the end of the Brythonic Celtic language in Scotland. Curnow – first found in west Cornwall in the 1560s – indicates that even at this date and in its West Cornish heartland, speaking the Cornish language was unusual. Inglis (and English) are found in Scotland to refer to English nationality. In this case the reference is to nationality, not language spoken.

STORY NICKNAMES

Just occasionally it is possible to wonder if a seemingly improbable story of a nickname origin really is correct. The Armstrong family claims that their surname comes from an action of their progenitor Fairbairn, squire and standard-bearer to King David I of Scots. In the Battle of the Standard (1138) the king's horse was killed under him, and the king's death seemed imminent, but Fairbairn rode up, picked him up with one arm, and rode to safety. Bearing in mind the light armour of the day (the full suits of armour familiar from countless films came later), the action is within the bounds of possibility for a man of exceptional strength. Additionally the origin of very many surnames within Scotland does date from the reign of David I. The story strikes me as plausible. Quite literally Fairbairn was the 'arm strong' who picked up the king and saved him from death. The subsequent role of the Armstrong family in defending the turbulent border region of the Solway Moss gives a reason to retain the name. Today the family has a motto canting on their name – *vi et armis invictus maneo* ('by strength and arms I remain unconquered'). The surname Armstrong has the unique distinction of being that of the first man to step on to the Moon: Neil Armstrong.

Figure 11. Armstrong is a nickname commemorating a courageous deed. It is appropriate for the surname of Neil Armstrong, the first man to walk on the Moon.

ACTIVITY

Assessing nicknames

▶ Would you give someone the nickname 'Brown' because they have brown hair? Is the characteristic which your possible nickname surname might commemorate sufficiently distinctive to be a plausible cause of a nickname?

▶ Surnames including Clod, Drunkard and Miser have been claimed to be of nickname origin. While nicknames are inflicted on people by those around them, there is a degree of choice in the adoption of a nickname by a family. Would you be happy to be known by such a nickname made into a surname?

▶ Can you see the nickname being a cause of pride for its early bearers? Names such as Palmer and Armstrong clearly pass this test.

If the surname you are looking at passes the tests above, it may be a nickname. If it doesn't then don't believe the surname dictionaries or internet sources that tell you to the contrary.

Take for example Drake. If you believe countless surname books it is a nickname for someone who looked like a duck. The characteristic is not sufficiently distinctive for it to be likely to become an enduring nickname. But let us set aside this problem – instead, would you be happy to be called Drake because someone applied this nickname to your father or grandfather? Probably not. Would you see it as a source of family pride that someone thought your ancestor resembled a duck? Surely not. Drake is almost certainly not a nickname. It has been suggested that it may be a place name, from Draknage Manor (Kingsbury, Warwickshire) – but it cannot be, as the surname is older than the house. Sir Francis Drake put forward a folk etymology for his name, that the surname means dragon. In Drake's age there was considerable interest in King Arthur, whose banner was (supposedly) a dragon, so Drake was in fact linking himself with the age of Arthur. It's a great story, but again almost certainly not quite right. In fact Drake is most probably an occupation name, from Norman French *drakere*, a standard bearer. This is a surname from a specific function within the Anglo-Norman army. Curiously Sir Francis Drake's etymology is not entirely wrong. The word *drakere* is ultimately linked to *dragon*, a beast once used on standards.

ACTIVITY

Investigating nicknames

A proper nickname investigation involves an examination of both the name and its cultural context. This is how it works: take for example Curnow as a nickname for a Cornish speaker. This can be investigated in the following steps.

▶ What is the earliest record? The first I can see is in the 1560s in the village of Mawgan on the Lizard peninsula.

▶ What does the spelling show? Curnow is an English spelling. In modern Cornish orthography it is Kernowek. The name is therefore being spelt by English people.

▶ What was happening to the Cornish language? While there were a very few speakers of Cornish as late as the end of the 18th century, the language effectively died in the first half of the 16th century. Curiously, language death is a rapid process, and two generations (about 60 years) is all it takes. By the 1560s speaking Cornish would have been noteworthy.

▶ Why was a surname needed? Cornish used a patronymic system (as Welsh did) so a Cornish speaker didn't actually have a surname, something which was an English-language feature – which no doubt caused problems for official records, e.g. parish registers.

▶ Why this particular name? Curnow is both an epithet and an explanation of why there wasn't a surname to put in the box. There is a parallel process with Scott (speaker of Scots Gaelic, hence a Scottish name, mainly Lowlands) and Wales/Welsh/Welch from the English counties bordering Wales and meaning Welsh-speaking. Also Wallace, a speaker of Strathclyde Welsh.

As it happens this surname provides an additional fragment of information to help date the decline of Cornish, and therefore to help understand the history of Cornwall. That being a Cornish speaker was a matter of note in the 1560s supports the established view that Cornish had substantially vanished by this date.

10

Working with the Genealogical Approach

In 1403 a mariner called Piers Rade, a Fleming from Dunkirk, was pursued by the French and rescued by mariners from Orford Ness in Suffolk. For this service the people of Orford Ness demanded payment, seizing his boat. Piers Rade petitioned the King of England, Henry IV, and the matter was decided by a formal process. The people of Orford Ness were ordered to return his boat, and Piers Rade was ordered to pay 40 shillings as the cost of his rescue. The records give no hint as to why Piers Rade decided to stay in England, but he did and thereby introduced his surname.

The original Flemish origin of the surname Rade is likely to be a place name. The name is found in Belgium today. What is fascinating is that we have a precise date and manner of its introduction into the British Isles. Records subsequent to 1403 are patchy, but the name turns up for example in Benenden, Kent in the mid-16th century. It was certainly well established. Yet today the name has almost vanished within the British Isles. Probably most bearers of the name accepted a drift from a foreign-sounding name – effectively *raad*, with a long *a* which is not really English in this position – to the familiar Reed. But for the genealogist we have a case of a name with a single point of origin, a few centuries of existence, and a gradual absorption within another surname.

TRACING A FIRST SURNAME BEARER

Common surnames are harder to trace than unusual surnames. However, progress can usually be made even with the most common names. Key guidance includes the following.

- All genealogy proceeds one step at a time – and careful generation by generation researching of a pedigree is the same process whether you are looking at Smith or an unusual surname.

- Help from living relatives can be particularly important with a common surname. In particular such help can reduce considerably your costs of research as you are in effect checking information which has been given rather than working with a multitude of possibilities.

- Local records are particularly important with a common surname. Often this means that a visit or visits to a local record office are essential.

- Researching common surnames will inevitably lead to blocks. In order to find work-arounds you need to research the family as widely as possible.

The requirements above in effect mean that researching a common surname will take longer and perhaps cost more than an uncommon name. Additionally because such lines are difficult and genealogists tend to do less with them, you will have less chance of linking with other people who happen to be interested in the same line.

There is a little good news – it gets easier the further back you go. Researching a family by the name of Jones through the 19th century is difficult. Mobility was such that many moved extensively. Tracking down a specific John Jones somewhere in the British Isles is challenging. Back in the 18th century it may well be easier. Probably a family is more rooted in a particular parish. Additionally those recording information were aware of the difficulty of distinguishing one John Jones from another, and were likely to give additional information to help identity. And in the 17th century it is easier still. For example, a line of Joneses in Smarden, Kent, is relatively straightforward to trace because the surname is rare for that location at that time.

A big area for genealogy in the next few years is work with the common surnames. Progress can be made on these names and inevitably will be made. Many may be found to have a large but nonetheless clearly limited number of points of origin, and a combination of genealogy and DNA may enable the surnames to be broken into a number of separate families. All – even Smith and Jones – must have a finite number of points of origin, and in time it may be possible to catalogue these.

ACTIVITY

Tracing a family line to its origin

This is by far the biggest activity of this book – tracing the line of your surname back to the time of its formation. In many cases this is possible (and several How To books will tell you how, including my own *Your Family Tree Online*) but it is a serious undertaking. Maybe it is best to think of this as a project over many years and in collaboration with others. It can be most satisfying.

11

Exploring 1066 Names

Before 1066, surnames were not used in the British Isles. Instead a first name alone sufficed to identify a person. Both the English and the Celts made use of a much larger first-name stock than we have today, and were far more ready to invent new names. Often families used naming conventions where similar sounding names were given to several children. So King Aethelwulf of Wessex named his sons Aethelstan, Aethelswift, Aethelbald, Aethelbert, Aethelred and Alfred – presumably by the time Alfred came along he had run out of names starting with Aethel–. In time King Alfred continued the tradition with sons Aethelflaed and Aethelweard, as well as daughters Aethelfleda and Aethelgifu. In Anglo-Saxon records we do sometimes see that someone was son or daughter of whomever, or have their occupation given or the name of the lands they owned, and we do see nicknames. But there is no suggestion that any of these were true surnames. Very many popular accounts of surnames suggest an Anglo-Saxon origin for a surname suggesting that the name is pre-Conquest – these cannot ever be defended.

1066 AND ALL THAT

Surnames in the British Isles start with the Normans. We do not have a list of all the names of the men who fought with William the Conqueror at the Battle of Hastings. But just 20 years later we do have the names of many of his Norman supporters listed in the Domesday Book of 1086. Here are recorded the Normans who had been granted confiscated English land, as well as the English who had managed to work with the Normans and so retained their land. We also find Norman names in a mass of charters and legal documents from the reign of King William I and his successors. A few of these Norman names are in the form of a first name plus a surname, with the surnames passing from father to child. They are therefore genuine surnames, and among the earliest in the British Isles.

Figure 12. Only one surname from the Battle of Hastings is known for sure – that of Malet. Most men were known by first name alone, as here – Bishop Odo, William and Robert from the Bayeux Tapestry.

Even before the Norman Conquest some Normans had surnames. Ralph de Tosny (believed to have fought at the Battle of Hastings) was the son of Roger de Tosny. This Roger was the son to *another* Ralph de Tosny, and he in turn was the son of yet *another* Ralph de Tosny, who lived around AD 950. In part the name reflects the inheritance of the Tosny estate, but its use over four generations begins to look very much like a surname. Notwithstanding, such early cases of surnames are rare. Rather it is in the British Isles in the late 11th century and throughout the 12th that the process accelerated. A reason was that Norman first names were by no means as prolific as either the Anglo-Saxon or Celtic first names, with a handful of names occurring again and again. This provided a pressure for some way other than a first name to identify a person.

The prefix 'de' of many Norman names has been retained with just a few. One of the strangest is Death, variously spelt Deeth, de'Ath(e) and even d'Eath(e). The surname is from the place Ath in modern Belgium and de Ath is therefore a regular formation. A problem with the surname is that if the prefix *de* is dropped, the remaining *Ath* sounds very like the English unstressed interrogative *eh?* so there was a good reason to retain the *de*.

NORMAN ENGLAND

William the Conqueror didn't have a surname. His lands were Normandy and his title that of the Duke of Normandy, but Normandy was not his surname. His grand-daughter Queen Matilda married Geoffrey of Plantagenet, Count of Anjou, and Plantagenet is used by their descendants as if a surname – and certainly we speak of the royal House of Plantagenet. Yet this name was slow to reach the permanence of a true surname.

Matilda's grandson is known to history as King Richard Coeur de Lion – only rarely as Richard Plantagenet. Perhaps kings didn't need surnames. But others certainly did.

We have some examples of the first surnames of Norman England. The major supporters of William the Conqueror in 1066, contributing ships or leading a section of his army were:

> Robert de Mortain
> Odo de Bayeux
> William d'Evreux
> Robert de Beaumont
> Roger de Montgomery
> Robert d'Eu
> William fitzOsbern
> Hugh de Avranches
> Hugh de Montfort
> Gerold the Seneschal
> Fulk d'Aunou
> Walter Giffard
> Nicholas, Abbot of St Ouen
> Eustace de Boulogne
> Alan Fergant

Of these 15 men, only one does not have a surname (Nicholas, Abbot of St Ouen). One has an occupation name (Gerold the Seneschal), one has a patronymic (William fitzOsbern) and two have surnames whose origin is not immediately obvious (Walter Giffard and Alan Fergant). Ten of the 15 have names which are in the form of place names and represent the estates or territories that they owned or ruled over.

Some of these names have entered the British surname stock. We certainly have today the surnames Montgomery, Osborn, de Montfort and Giffard, and it is possible that bearers of these names are descendants of the nobles who supported William at the Battle of Hastings. However, the majority of the surnames on this list have not become part of the mainstream of British surnames. It seems that the surnames were as durable as the French estates they represented and that when the families living in England lost control of these estates, they also lost their surnames. What we are seeing is the very beginnings of surnames within the British Isles, a time when surnames were just beginning to become fixed but were not yet truly fixed.

Names in the Domesday Book

We also find evidence of Norman names, including a few surnames, in the Domesday Book (1086). A key concept is that while surnames certainly exist by 1086 they are still rare. Typical Domesday Book entries are as the following (all from Sussex) and all showing first names alone:

> Sullington. Wulfward held it from king Edward.
>
> Ralph holds Wiston from (king) William. Azor held it from earl Godwin.
>
> William son of Mann holds Wappingthorne from (king) William. Karl held it from king Edward.

Just occasionally a place name is shown as what appears to be a surname, for example:

> Geoffrey de Flocques holds Guestling from the count.
>
> Robert de Hastings holds 2 ½ hides of this manor from the abbot.

Most of these nascent surnames are from Normandy, Brittany or Flanders though a very few are from England, as in de Hastings.

NORMAN BRITISH ISLES

While there is a tendency to associate the Norman Conquest with England, it soon became a conquest of the whole of the British Isles. The Norman concept of surnames was spread with their conquest.

In 1072 Scotland was invaded by the Anglo-Normans, an army of both English and Norman troops commanded by officers mostly Norman, with King William I of England himself riding as far north as the Firth of Tay. King Malcolm III of Scots paid homage to William, starting a period of centuries when Scotland was to a greater or lesser extent a fiefdom of the Anglo-Normans. Scotland moved decisively into the Norman cultural orbit during the reign of King David I of Scots (1124–1153). It is from David's reign that most of the oldest Scottish surnames date, with many seemingly formed around the time of the Battle of the Standard (1138).

The Welsh border counties of England were given into the care of some of King William I's most trusted barons, and from these bases Wales was subject to a long and drawn-out process of piecemeal conquest and colonization. Much of Wales was in Norman hands by the mid-12th century, though the formal invasion of Wales under King Edward I dates from 1282. In contrast with England, Scotland and Ireland, Wales retained its own distinctive naming system based around patronymics, with Norman-style surnames associated with just a very few families there.

The Anglo-Norman invasion of Ireland (from Wales) dates from 1169, with subsequent progressive tightening of Norman control. From 1199 the titles of King of England and Lord of Ireland were inherited together. As part of the Norman cultural impact, Ireland adopted Norman-style surnames.

For the majority of the great age of surname formation the countries of the British Isles were under *de facto* Norman rule. Among the islands, the Channel Islands were an integral part of the dukedom of Normandy, attached with this title to the English crown, while the Isle of Man and the Western and Northern Isles of Scotland were under Norse rule. As Norse rule waned in these territories, Norman surname practices entered. It is as a result of the Norman conquest of all of the British Isles that a relatively uniform pattern of surnames is found throughout.

ACTIVITY

The Battle Abbey Roll

A source which claims to be a list of Norman surnames brought to Britain in 1066 is the *Battle Abbey Roll*, available online from the National Library of Scotland at **www.nls.uk/auchinleck/**

Unfortunately this source is not what it claims to be. Rather it is a 16th-century printed source which may possibly derive from a 14th-century document. This *Battle Abbey Roll* has been shown by scholarly attention in the 19th century and subsequently to be at earliest a 14th-century compilation, and quite possibly not even that early.

Notwithstanding, the *Battle Abbey Roll* has value for surname studies. It indicates the surnames that people in an earlier age – perhaps as early as the 14th century – thought of as Norman names. It was compiled at a time when most of the nobility were indeed of Norman French origin and many of them still French-speaking, or had only recently given up speaking French. While it would be wrong to claim that a name in the

Battle Abbey Roll is the name of a soldier who fought with William Duke of Normandy at the Battle of Hastings, it is reasonable to see it as a list of the names of Norman families living in England. And presumably some of the names on the *Battle Abbey Roll* were indeed present at the Battle of Hastings.

Of the soldiers of the Battle of Hastings (as opposed to the Norman nobles who backed the conquest) only a single name is known with certainty, that of William Malet. Almost everything we know about him is from later records, though there is no particular reason to disbelieve it. He was of Norman and English parentage and the uncle of Edith, wife of King Harold II of England – so he had ties with both sides of the battle. After the battle he buried his niece's husband, the slain King Harold II. King William I made him first high sheriff of Yorkshire, and later sheriff of Suffolk, with extensive lands in the county. Malet has the distinction of being the oldest surname in the British Isles. Descent from William Malet can be demonstrated by some families. The Malet family and the royal family are the only two where a line back to the Battle of Hastings can actually be shown – and Malet is the only proven continuously used surname.

12

Understanding Coats of Arms and Surnames

Coats of arms came into existence throughout Europe in the 12th century and were firmly established within a century. As with surnames, a coat of arms passes from father to children, and the association between coats of arms and surnames is strong.

The right to bear a coat of arms is legally controlled. Just because your surname is the same as a family that has a coat of arms doesn't mean you are entitled to bear it. Indeed, throughout the UK you are actually breaking the law if you display such arms as if they relate to you. In Scotland, imprisonment may result, at least in theory. Every heraldic scroll, key fob and surname history which bears a coat of arms is selling something which – if displayed – is technically illegal. The large industry both in the UK and North America around scrolls of 'family' coats of arms and crests is a fraud and is thoroughly distasteful.

If you can prove direct descent in the male line from someone who had a coat of arms, you may be able to bear it, though you still need to get it formally registered to you through the appropriate heraldic body and have appropriate modifications made to distinguish it from other branches of the family. The position is more relaxed in the Irish Republic. There, if you can prove descent from a sept (family) bearing a coat of arms, you may use the arms 'without any impropriety' as they are 'by custom regarded as appertaining to all members of a sept' (Edward McLysaght, Ireland's First Chief Herald).

ARMS REFLECT SURNAMES

Sometimes coats of arms show devices appropriate to the origin of the surname. Thus the coat of arms of the Palmer family of Howlets, Kent, shows awareness that their ancestor was a palmer, a word which meant specifically a Jerusalem pilgrim, and shows three palmers' scripts (pilgrims' bags). Their Somerset descendants added a pilgrim's staff.

Frequently coats of arms are puns on the surname of the bearer, a process called *canting*. Thus for example the Sharpey family of Kent bore arms which showed three spears, a pun on the word *sharp* as a (now obsolete) term for a sharp weapon. In fact the surname is most probably a place name in origin (probably the Isle of Sheppey, itself the 'island of sheep') and has nothing to do with a spear, but presumably spears were seen as more 'heraldic' than sheep! Several coats of arms are associated with different Mills families, one of which – that for Mills of Norton Court, Kent – includes a *millrind*, the iron centre piece of a grindstone. Certainly this family are playing up the association with milling, though whether in reference to a known mill owner as an ancestor or simply as an example of canting is not clear. Aherne is an Irish surname (centred in Co. Limerick and Co. Clare) with an Irish-language origin, but this fact has not prevented the heralds finding a canting reference based on the English words *a hern*, where hern is the archaic form of 'heron'. Thus an Aherne family has a coat of arms bearing a heron. It is hard to escape the view that canting is less the art of punning and more the art of bad punning.

Mr. Justice Rooth.

Figure 13. A coat of arms for a member of the Rooth family with a motto canting on the surname.

Coats of arms can hint at links between families otherwise lost. The stork is quite an unusual heraldic bird, yet it is born on the coats of arms of at least eight Gibson families: in London (two families), Essex, Yorkshire, Lancashire, Northumberland, Cumberland and Ireland. This circumstance strongly suggests that all these families, and perhaps therefore all with the surname Gibson, are in fact related, and this relationship was known to the families when they were granted their arms. Gibson is a patronymic (son of Gilbert) with the earliest record seemingly Henry Gibsonne in Nottinghamshire in 1311. It is plausible that this Henry Gibsonne is the sole progenitor of all Gibson families and that he used a stork as his (now lost) heraldic symbol, a circumstance remembered by eight descendants in different branches.

MOTTOS AND SURNAMES

Mottos can relate to the surname. At least two Palmer families have used the motto *palma virtuti*, ('the palm of virtue') which refers to the Jerusalem pilgrim's palm frond from which their name derives. Sometimes families use mottos which sound like their name. For example, the Elliott family of Stroud has *cum aliis pro aliis* (with others for others), a motto where the sound of the Latin words seems more important than its meaning. Sometimes the relevance of a motto to a surname is less obvious. Rooth echoes two semi-archaic English words, *wroth* and *ruth*, both of whose meanings are modified in the motto 'dare and bear'.

ACTIVITY

Your coat of arms
The College of Arms (England, Wales and Northern Ireland) and Court of Lord Lyon (Scotland) are still active in granting coats of arms. If you are an upstanding citizen of the United Kingdom there is absolutely no reason why you should not obtain a coat of arms. Worthy foreign nationals of British descent may also be made a grant of arms though the process is usually as an honour rather than in response to a request. The process of drawing and registering coats of arms has costs attached (in the thousands of pounds) but is otherwise straightforward. A coat of arms may serve as a personal identifier, perhaps in connection with a business, or may be a noteworthy present for a retiring entrepreneur. Grants of arms often reflect the careers of the individuals for whom they are granted. Sometimes they reflect the surname also. And of course they are heirlooms, inherited in the male line (with appropriate registration in each generation).

The Republic of Ireland is covered by the office of the Chief Herald of Ireland. Local arrangements apply to the Channel Islands and Isle of Man.

13

Orphans and Surnames

There is an entry from the parish register of Brotherton, Yorkshire, which records a Christening in the following terms:

> 1651 Roger the sonne of I know not who was baptised I know not when.

Presumably Roger must have adopted a surname. But we cannot know what it might have been. There is no fixed process by which orphans adopt surnames.

ORPHANS OF THE VICTORIAN AGE

The Victorian age had no established method of assigning surnames to foundlings. The process was handled by the overseers of the poor – therefore at a local level – and often in a cavalier fashion. The lack of system is described by Charles Dickens in *Oliver Twist* through the words of the beadle, Mr Bumble:

> 'Notwithstanding the most superlative, and, I may say, super-nat'ral exertions on the part of this parish,' said Bumble, 'we have never been able to discover who is his father, or what was his mother's settlement, name or condition.'
>
> Mrs. Mann raised her hands ... 'How comes he to have any name at all then?'
>
> The beadle drew himself up with great pride, and said, 'I invented it ... We name our foundlings in alphabetical order. The

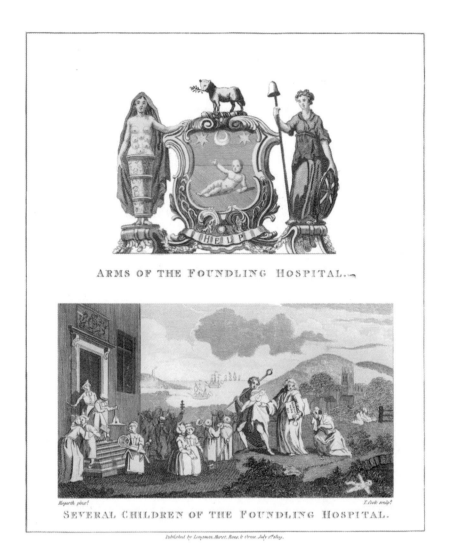

ARMS OF THE FOUNDLING HOSPITAL.

SEVERAL CHILDREN OF THE FOUNDLING HOSPITAL.

Figure 14. One of the many problems confronting foundlings of the 18th and 19th centuries was the lack of a surname.

last was a S, — Swubble, I named him. This was a T, — Twist, I named him. The next one as comes will be Unwin and the next Zwilkins...'

A concern may have been to avoid any surname which existed in the parish or the vicinity (and therefore implied paternity), a circumstance which may have led to the creation of truly whimsical forms. *Oliver Twist* hints at this – Swubble and Zwilkins are (as far as I can tell) not in fact British Isles surnames. Sometimes foundlings were named after the village, the dedication of the parish church, the street in which they had been found, or even given the surname Found.

ACTIVITY

Orphans and surnames

This is a difficult area to investigate and it may well be that appropriate records are just not available. However, there are some avenues to be explored.

▶ Family traditions can be particularly important. If the orphan is one of your ancestors and your line has remembered nothing about their origins, consider contacting cousins who may have that all-important oral history.

▶ Message boards on genealogy websites are particularly useful in resolving blocks around orphans and posting on an appropriate forum is recommended.

▶ Both birth certificates and christening records should be consulted for possible name variants or alternatives.

▶ An extensive list of sources for investigating the lives and families of orphans is found online on Cyndi's List **www.cyndislist.com/ orphans.htm**

14

English Surnames

More than half of English surnames are from place names. And conversely, most British Isles place-name surnames are from England. For the remainder of English surnames, location names are common – and of course many of these are reduced forms of place names. Trade names are a significant category in England. By contrast patronymics, while they are certainly found in England, are far less common than other types. Names from nicknames are most unusual.

There are regional variants. Most of the few English patronymics are from the North East or the South. Yorkshire scarcely uses patronymics (rather place names and occupational names comprise almost the whole of the surname stock). And Cornwall as a county with a Celtic heritage is a special case.

PARISH REGISTERS AND SURNAMES

The stabilization of the English surname system is closely linked with the development of the parish register system. Parish registers recorded the christening, marriage and burial of every member of the community irrespective of class. The system invited conformity – a child should be christened with the same surname as that which their father gave on his marriage; at marriage bride and groom should show the same name as at christening; a burial should show the same name as marriage and christening.

There were sporadic records akin to parish registers through the late medieval period – for example, some priests noted christenings and burials on the flyleaf or even occasionally in the margins of their service book. The driving force for the introduction of parish registers was a 1497 requirement by the Spanish Cardinal Ximenes of Toledo that throughout Christendom all christenings should be recorded. Many European countries adopted some form of parish registers shortly thereafter, and from the beginning the practice was wider than Ximenes's list of Christenings, recording also marriages and burials. The very earliest English parish register records appear to be from Alfriston, Sussex, where records of marriages start from 1504.

Parish registers and the parish chest

Within England the real start of parish registers is 1538 when Thomas Cromwell ordered that every christening, wedding and burial should be recorded in a book stored in a 'secure coffer' with two locks, and with a system of fines for parishes that did not keep this requirement. By doing this Cromwell in effect introduced both the parish register and the parish chest which kept them safe, and which came to be used to store a mass of parish papers. From 1598 a register of better quality was required, along with the statement that entries from 1538 'but especially from the first year of her Majesty's reign' (i.e. the first year of Queen Elizabeth I's reign, 1558) should be copied into it. Most extant early parish registers in England are from 1598 with transcripts of the previous 40 or 60 years.

The process of transcription meant that the incumbent of 1598 became familiar with the forms of surnames recorded in his parish for the previous one to three generations. Earlier forms were that much closer to their ultimate origin, and may reasonably be expected to use a form which reflected earlier pronunciation and perceived etymology. The process was in effect one of archaising surnames for the present generation, so many of the forms used in entries from 1598 may already have been old-fashioned.

MULTI-WORD SURNAMES

England makes particular use of multi-word surnames, a formation which can be regarded as typically English. These fall into two categories:

- verb plus noun, as in Shakespeare;
- adjective plus noun, as in Longfellow.

Shakespeare has several similar forms: Shakeshaft, Shakelance, Shakespur and perhaps even Shacklock and Shaxsted, as well as spelling variants of all these. In origin these are occupational names, meaning simply a spearman in the army. It is possible that they are all effectively the same name, with spear, shaft, lance and spur perceived as synonyms. Similarly, Longfellow and Longman may be the same name in origin. It may be that in the early generations of surnames such as these the meaning of the two-word combination was remembered. Within this mind-set Shakespeare and Shakeshaft or Longfellow and Longman would have been perceived not as different names but as forms of the same name.

MIGRANT SURNAMES

England has absorbed many groups of migrants, and their names.

One of the biggest groups is the Huguenots, French Protestants who migrated to England. In 1572 in the St Bartholomew's Day massacre around 70,000 Huguenots were slaughtered on the orders of the French King Charles IX, with many of the survivors fleeing to England and the Netherlands. For those who remained in France, a degree of religious tolerance was established in France by the 1598 Edict of Nantes, but its revocation in 1685 once again made the Huguenots subject to persecution. England therefore received two influxes of fleeing Huguenots nearly a century apart, in the 1570s and 1680s. Both waves arrived with French surnames, and both quickly anglicized them. The 1570s migrants have left less trace of this process as the parish register system was just starting, but the 1680s wave has often left a trail which shows a French surname developing into what seems to be an English surname. Thus a family with the surname Hervé in the 1680s becomes Harvey by the 1690s.

Many Jewish migrants came to Britain from 1657, following an announcement by Oliver Cromwell that the 1290 decree expelling Jews from Britain had no relevance. By around 1690 there were in the region of 3,000 Jews in England. The migrants were the Jewish Sephardim from Spain and Portugal fleeing the Inquisition, and they brought with them the surnames of Iberia.

Migrants from Scotland, Wales and Northern Ireland feature strongly within the surname stock of the English cities. An illustration is provided by the iconic group The Beatles from England's Liverpool. The four musicians of The Beatles were all Liverpool born and bred, and may therefore be expected to have English surnames from the vicinity of Liverpool. George Harrison almost does – Harrison is a north of England surname, though mainly from the North East (Liverpool is North West). Yet his ancestry is by no means restricted to England but including the surname Frenches, an Anglo-Norman surname for someone of Norman French origin brought to Ireland (County Wexford) during the Anglo-Norman Conquest – and brought from Ireland to

Liverpool in the 19th century. Ringo Starr – the alias of Richard Starkey – shows in Starkey a Celtic name brought from Ireland to many English cities (though his recent ancestry was in the Liverpool area). John Lennon's surname is an anglicization of the

Figure 15. The Beatles from England's city of Liverpool. Only one has an English surname, and even that is not from Liverpool.

Irish surname O'Lennain, common in Counties Cork, Fermanagh and Galway – while his ancestry includes the Irish surnames Gidea and McGuires. Paul McCartney's surname hints at distant Scottish ancestry, though McCartney is most frequently encountered in Ulster. His mother's maiden name Mohin is a variant of Mohan, from County Monaghan.

The cities of England are something of a melting pot for surnames from throughout the British Isles as well as from further afield.

CORNWALL

Cornish, the ancient language of Cornwall, is a Celtic language most closely related to Welsh and Breton. The Celtic language became extinct in the 18th century after a long period of decline. Cornwall's Celtic heritage is strongly reflected in its place names; surnames, however, show primarily English forms.

Patronymics scarcely exist within the Cornish name-stock. This situation stands in stark contrast with Wales, where patronymics are almost the only source of surnames, and Scotland and Ireland where patronymics are very common. In theory Cornwall should yield surnames beginning *map–* or *ap–*, or surnames which are in the form of an English final *–s* or *–son*. In practice I cannot find such names associated with Cornwall. The paucity of patronymic surnames demonstrates that in most areas the Cornish language had passed from common use before the creation of surnames, effectively therefore well before the 14th century. Rather Cornwall adopted the standard English practice of creating surnames from place names or trades.

The trade names are essentially the same as those found elsewhere in England. There are a few specifically Cornish forms, for example Gloyne for a charcoal burner using a Cornish word for this trade (though a word which probably entered into the Cornish dialect of English, so it is a regional English dialect word which gave rise to the surname, not a Cornish word). Names from place names are often formed from places that were in origin Cornish language names, and therefore sound very Cornish. They reflect the Cornish place names prevalent in Cornwall. There is a much quoted rhyme which reminds us:

> By Ros, Car, Lan, Tre, Pol and Pen
> Ye may know most Cornishmen.

Indeed this is correct – the majority of distinctive Cornish names contain these elements, with the last three, Tre, Pol and Pen, being especially common, reflecting the frequency of these elements within Cornish place names. The most common place-name elements, all of which may be found in Cornish surnames, are:

ros – heathland
car – carn, fort, camp
lan – enclosure
tre – homestead
pol – pond or well
pen – headland

A particular feature of Cornwall is that some curious angliciza-
tions of Cornish names have developed. Thus Carnebwen (a place
name) became the surname Kneebone.

ACTIVITY

From the age of Magna Carta
Printed and online histories of the high Middle Ages are a great source
for surname research.

Take for example the Magna Carta of 1215. This foundation document
of the English constitution and of English common law has many
witnesses, given evidence of the state of English surnames in the early
13th century. For example, these are the barons:

Gilbert de Clare, heir to the earldom of Hertford.
John FitzRobert, Lord of Warkworth Castle.
Robert FitzWalter, Lord of Dunmow Castle.
William de Fortibus, Earl of Albemarle.
William Hardel, Mayor of the City of London.
William de Huntingfield, Sheriff of Norfolk and Suffolk.
John de Lacy, Lord of Pontefract Castle.
William de Lanvallei, Lord of Standway Castle.
William Malet, Sheriff of Somerset and Dorset.
Geoffrey de Mandeville, Earl of Essex and Gloucester.
William Marshall Jr, heir to the earldom of Pembroke.
Roger de Montbegon, Lord of Hornby Castle, Lancashire.
Richard de Montfichet, Baron.

William de Mowbray, Lord of Axholme Castle.
Richard de Percy, Baron.
Saire de Quincy, Earl of Winchester.
Robert de Roos, Lord of Hamlake Castle.
Geoffrey de Saye, Baron.
Robert de Vere, heir to the earldom of Oxford.
Eustace de Vesci, Lord of Alnwick Castle.

Every one of these barons has a surname. Many of these are recognizable names of today: Claire (and Sinclair), Hardy, Lacy, Malet, Mandeville (and Manville), Marshall, Montfichet, Mowbray, Percy, de Vere. It is perfectly practical to comb the history of the high Middle Ages for instances of surnames you are interested in. A trip to a library will pay dividends. Search engines reveal much.

ACTIVITY

The National Archives

England has an incredible richness of documents from the Middle Ages – more than any other part of the British Isles, and more than most countries in Europe. Surnames are recorded in profusion, and any of the mass of documents can be used as a source of information on surnames. Remarkably, much of the documentary heritage of England is now available at the click of a mouse from the National Archives' *Documents Online* at **www.nationalarchives.gov.uk/documents online/**

It is as simple as entering a surname. Hits are grouped according to the type of record so it is easy to select early or recent. Very many people of no particular wealth or power are recorded, providing an early record of their surnames.

Documents Online is particularly strong for English documents but it additionally includes much that is relevant for Wales, Scotland and Ireland.

15

Welsh Surnames

Wales is the land of the patronym. The country has a very long patronymic tradition, and today almost all Welsh surnames are derived from patronyms. A feature of the Welsh system was – and to a limited extent still is today in Welsh-speaking areas – the custom of listing more than one generation within a patronymic, creating what is in effect a pedigree. A Welsh-speaking Welsh child learning their own name learns their ancestry, usually for six or seven generations, a feat unusual in England.

Wales did come under Anglo-Norman control, and there are some instances of Norman surnames forming in Wales, for example FitzGerald. However – in contrast with Scotland and Ireland – the pre-existing patronymic system continued largely unchanged.

PATRONYMICS

The Welsh patronymic system developed alongside unique Welsh legal conventions, reflecting an independent legal tradition which once existed. While Wales lost its independent criminal law following the death of King Llewelyn the Last (1282), its independent civil law continued much longer – until 1536 – while arbitration using Welsh concepts continued even into the 17th century. The law in Wales made knowing a pedigree a virtual necessity.

■ Land mostly passed from father to sons, with each receiving an equal share. The youngest had the task of dividing the land, with each brother selecting their portion in turn and the youngest getting the last piece remaining. Land left to anyone other than the sons could be contested by them and their heirs at intervals of four years for four generations. A man could dispute the distribution of the estate of his great-grandfather.

■ *Compurgation* was the means by which most disputes were settled. A defendant would take an oath which was then supported by a number of people who swore that they believed the oath. These people had to be unrelated to the defendant – and had to know that they were unrelated.

For both land law and dispute resolution, knowing your pedigree was essential.

The Welsh system strings together the names of a family with an elliptic form of *mab*, meaning *son of* – a form related to Scottish and Irish *mac*. While there is some variation in the shortened form of *mab* used, it is usually *ab–* before a vowel and *ap–* before a consonant, giving rise to forms such as *ab-Owen*, son of Owen, and *ap-Hugh*, son of Hugh. The comparable form for a woman is *verch* (in modern orthography *ferch*), which gives rise to such forms as *verch-Owen* and *verch-Hugh*. On marriage women retain their own names.

Names within the Welsh system were inevitably long, with long pedigrees remembered. A name was proverbially 'as long as a Welshman's pedigree'. While nicknames were very frequently used (and indeed are still very frequent in Wales), they were never (or almost never) the catalyst for surname formation.

From Patronymic to Surname

Surnames were slow coming to Wales. The pedigree patronymics simply made surnames unnecessary. With very rare exceptions – usually of English migrant families – there are (almost) no surnames in Wales before the Act of Union (1536) and very few before the early 17th century. Even looking at Hearth Tax Returns of the 1670s it can be seen that most people used a Welsh patronymic rather than an English-style surname.

The first Welsh surnames were formed in the parts of Wales adjacent to England (particularly Radnorshire) or were adopted by Welshmen who moved to England. By the early 17th century Jones was well established in England as a surname taken by migrants from Wales, yet Wales itself had not yet seen the wholesale adoption that has made the surname so prolific.

When surnames started to be formed in Wales it was inevitable that patronymics should predominate. About 95% of the surnames that can be identified as coming from Wales are securely classified as patronymics. Indeed non-patronymic surnames are so rare that it becomes reasonable to look with caution on all proposed alternatives and wonder if they are truly Welsh. For practical purposes the surnames that emerged in Wales in the 17th and 18th centuries were patronymics.

Most of the earliest formations are simply the father's name used without modification. Meredith, Morgan and Owen are widespread examples of this type. David and John are also found as early surnames, though both share a curious restricted distribution within Carmarthenshire and neighbouring districts. These are early formations; by contrast, most Welsh surnames were formed in the 17th and 18th centuries alongside the adoption of English as a second or first language. An individual would retain their Welsh generational patronymic when speaking in Welsh but use an English form of their name when speaking in English. The vast majority of these patronymics are therefore English language patronymics, names with a final –s (or occasionally –son) rather than prefixed ab–/ap–. The surnames formed reflected the Christian names of boys fashionable in Wales at this period, a strikingly restricted group. The main ones, in order, are as follows.

John	Jones
William	Williams
David	Davies
Thomas	Thomas
Evan	Evans
Robert	Roberts
Hugh	Hughes
Llywelyn	Lewis
Edward	Edwards
Maurice	Morris
James	James
Phillip	Phillips
Gruffyd	Griffiths

Many of these names are familiar from the English name stock. Hugh is English (and Norman) in origin but now largely forgotten in England, but Evan, Llywelyn and Gruffyd are almost exclusively Welsh. The high position of David represents the popularity of the patron saint of Wales, St David. Maurice is surprising as this English first name has never enjoyed particularly enduring popularity either in England or Wales; rather it seems to have been popular just at the time when surnames were being formed.

Wales has also produced many patronymics which are based on unusual first names. Thus Onions is from Ennion, an established (though not particularly common) Welsh first name. Occasionally surnames were formed from diminutives of first names. Thus the first name Maredudd has the diminutive Bedo, which has produced the surname Beddoes. Likewise Madog has the diminutive Mady and the surname Maddy. A frequently encountered part of a Welsh patronym is the adjective *bychan* (younger), which mutates as *fychan*, and is used to distinguish son from father. The form *fychan* passed into English as Vaughan, with variants including Baughan, Baugh, Vane and Bawn, demonstrating the difficulty English speakers find in pronouncing *fychan*.

Names formed from the mother's name – metronyms – are rare in Welsh but they do exist. They may be simply the mother's name, often with an anglicized spelling, as Gwenlan (from Gwenillan) and Gainor (from Gaenor). However, they can also come from the mother's patronymic, so verch-Richard gives rise to Critchett, and verch-Edward gives rise to Kedward.

WELSH OCCUPATION NAMES

Occupational surnames are very rare indeed. The occupation *saer* (carpenter) produces Saer. Similarly *gwas* (servant) has produced Wace. This last hints at the formation of these surnames. Wace is particularly associated with Shrewsbury, outside Wales but with many Welsh people working there, particularly in menial jobs. It may well be that this is a name applied by an English community that had some knowledge of Welsh, rather than a true home-grown Welsh surname. Saer has a Welsh distribution in that it appears mainly in Pembrokeshire and Carmarthenshire, yet this was an area with a substantial English-speaking population. It may well be that Saer, like Wace, should be regarded as an occupation name within the English tradition.

Place-name surnames

Welsh place names as sources of surnames are certainly to be found, but in England, Scotland and Ireland, not Wales. Thus Cardiff is recorded in Bristol in the 13th century and today is localized in Liverpool and Aberdeen. While the progenitor presumably came from Cardiff, the surname is in formation English and Scots, not Welsh. Similarly, the region Gwynedd has given rise to the English surname Whinnett. The Anglo-Norman invasion of Ireland was launched from Pembrokeshire, and took a string of place names from Pembrokeshire and Glamorganshire to Ireland: Prendergast, Carey and Barry have survived in Ireland. There are early examples of English place names being used as surnames by people living in Wales, but it is most likely that these names were the surnames of migrants from England to Wales and brought to Wales ready-made.

Nickname surnames

So few Welsh nicknames are known to have transferred into surnames that it is prudent to look with particular care at the few possible examples we have. Of these the best known is Lloyd – and its variants Floyd and Flood. There is a Welsh adjective *llwyd* meaning both grey and brown which is sometimes put forward as the origin. Yet why such an obscure nickname should give rise to one of the most common Welsh surnames is far from clear. The idea that it is a reference to hair colour seems extremely weak as neither brown nor grey is a particularly distinctive colour. Probably the best answer is that for the moment a convincing etymology for Lloyd cannot be offered. Much the same thinking applies to Mellon and its variant Melling, which appear to be from *melyn*, meaning yellow (not fair or blonde), but which is sometimes claimed to represent a hair colour. Baugh is also put forward as a Welsh nickname made a surname, from the adjective *bach* meaning small – yet it seems much more likely that it is a variant of Vaughan. The working hypothesis may be advanced that Wales has produced so few examples of surnames derived from nicknames that those few apparent possibilities need to be looked at with great scepticism.

SURNAMES IN SHORT SUPPLY

Today Wales is characterized by a paucity of surnames, a phenomenon unchanged since surnames were formed. In 1856 the Registrar-General, George Graham, estimated that nine-tenths of the population of Wales was covered by less than a hundred names. In Penllyn registration district (Merionethshire), 30% of the population had the surname Jones, while Wales as a whole had this surname for around 14% of its population. Today in the region of one man in 30 in Wales is called John Jones, while the top ten surnames in Wales are the surnames of 56% of the population of Wales. Because there aren't so very many of them, Welsh surnames score very highly in lists of the most common British or English surnames.

Getting to grips with Welsh surnames
A starting point is to categorize the Welsh surname.

▶ Does the name represent an early migrant from Wales to another part of the British Isles? Surnames in this category include Prendergast (to Ireland) and Cardiff (to England and Scotland). Surnames such as these may be best regarded as Irish, English or Scots as that is where they took root – and it really does seem to be the case that Cardiff is not in any meaningful sense a Welsh surname.

▶ Does the name represent a migrant (usually to England) before most surnames were formed in Wales? Among the earliest cases of the surname Jones are those that arose in England as a migrant from Wales was forced to take a surname (though there are plenty of subsequent Welsh Joneses).

▶ Is the name in fact not Welsh at all? Popularly Davis is often believed to be Welsh, though its distribution shows it to be far more common in England than Wales.

▶ Is the name Welsh? Can it be linked with a family, perhaps Welsh-speaking, or Welsh-speaking in recent generations?

Only the final group holds true Welsh surnames, the other groups being better understood within the surnaming practices of other parts of the British Isles.

Welsh names and Welsh culture
Welsh surnames in English are cross-cultural adaptations reflecting different languages and different naming systems. A true Welsh surname is either born alongside a Welsh-language patronymic name (which the bearer may well regard as their 'real' name) or was at some

stage the surname of an ancestor who had a Welsh language patronymic.

If you bear a Welsh surname and are a Welsh speaker you are clearly attached to the culture of Wales of which your surname is a part. For those who bear a Welsh surname but have lost this Welsh heritage, a goal might be to learn enough Welsh to say 'my name is . . .' and express their name in Welsh. The recent resurgence of the Welsh language means that Welsh-language instruction abounds: online, through books, CDs and DVDs, through classes, even through an Open University course.

Welsh culture is similarly flourishing. The National Eisteddfod festival of literature, music and the performing arts was established in 1860 and is now at the front of the Welsh cultural advance. A visit to a festival is a great way of experiencing the culture associated with a Welsh surname. The National Eisteddfod will be in Wrexham (2011) and the Vale of Glamorgan (2012).

16

Scottish Surnames

The Celtic tradition of patronymic usage existed in Scotland at least from the invasion of the Scots (who came from Ireland). The semi-legendary first king of Scots, Kenneth MacAlpin (810–853), displays the familiar patronymic form suggesting a father called Alpin. But MacAlpin is not a surname and is not born by Kenneth's son who reigned as King Constantine (862–877) – rather he is Constantine MacKenneth, and his son King Donald (889–900) was Donald MacConstantine.

EARLY SURNAMES

While the patronymic system is ancient, the earliest true surnames are not from patronymics. A collection of some of the earliest surnames of Scotland is given by William Stewart writing about 1535, who attributes their formation to the Council of Forfar (1061) when he says King Malcolm Canmore directed chiefs to take surnames from their lands. The date is implausibly early; indeed in a nutshell the date is simply wrong, but what William Stewart has given us is a list of surnames which were perceived in his time as being among the earliest. Stewart tells us that more or less at that time many surnames were made that did not exist before:

Mony surename also les and moir,
Wes maid that tyme quhilk wes nocht of befoir.
As Calder, Lokart, Gordoun, and Setoun,
Gallows, Lauder, Wawane, and Libertoun,
Meldrum, Schaw, Leirmond, and Cargill,
Stratherne, Rattray, Dundas als thairtill,
With Cokburne, Mar, and Abircrumby,
Myretoun, Menzeis, and also Leslie.

While the spellings may be a little strange, this is a list of surnames which stands at the bedrock of Scottish history. Scots orthography used both W and Z for the sound we would today write as G, so Wawane is Gavin and Menzeis is pronounced 'Mingis' though still spelt today with the archaic Z as Menzies. Stewart appears to have no source and his date seems to be around a century too early but he does manage to identify many of the earliest surnames of Scotland, and he rightly realizes that they are place names from the lands owned by the bearers.

THE ARRIVAL OF SURNAMES IN SCOTLAND

Surnames were no more than a generation or two later arriving in Scotland than in England. In Scotland as in England they were a characteristic of the ruling Norman elite. While William Stewart's date of 1061 is wrong we can nonetheless point to early origin, and fix the date to within a generation. Surnames came to Scotland during the reign of King David I (1124–1153). David grew up in England at the court of the English King Henry I and absorbed the Anglo-Norman values of the English nobility. His accession to the throne of Scotland began a process of anglicizing (or perhaps 'normanizing') of Scottish society. To King David is credited such steps as the foundation of many towns (burghs)

within Scotland, numerous monastic foundations and establishment of an Anglo-Norman governmental system – and all fostered
by an influx of Anglo-Norman rulers from England and
Normandy. The sort of changes that had occurred in England
from 1066 occurred in Scotland from 1124.

From the time of King David onwards the towns of Scotland were
multicultural. Thus around the 1150s the town of St Andrews in
Fife had four distinct communities: Scots, French (i.e. Normans),
Flemings and English. This was the cultural mix which created the
earliest Scottish surnames, most of which are surnames used by
migrants to Scotland rather than surnames of Scots.

The Ragman Rolls

An early snapshot of Scottish surnames is provided by the Ragman
Rolls of 1291 and 1296, the rolls recording the oaths of loyalty to
English King Edward I sworn by the nobility of Scotland. About
2000 surnames are recorded, representing almost all of the nobility
of Scotland. There are only a few dozen 'Macs' among them. At this
time being a noble and therefore having a surname was still very
much a feature of the Anglo-Norman ascendancy.

The Ragman Rolls include Edward I's client King John Balliol as
'Johannes de Balliolo dominus Galwidie', (John of Balliol Lord
Galloway) and Robert the Bruce who replaced him (and who
likewise swore allegiance to Edward I) as 'Robertus de Brus comes
de Carryk' (Robert of Bruce, Count of Carrick). Curiously a
phonetic memory of the 'de' has been preserved in the name by
which he is popularly remembered, 'Robert the Bruce' – for a
more accurate process of translation gives 'Robert of Bruce' (i.e.
Bruges). The line of the future house of Stuart is represented by
'Phelipp Stiward del counte de Rokesburgh' – Phillip, steward of

the county of Roxburgh, an example of one of the rare occupational names in the Ragman Rolls. The family of freedom fighter William Wallace is represented by 'Johan le Waleys fiz Thomas le Waleys del counte de Fyf' – John the Wallace son of Thomas the Wallace of the county of Fife. From 'Dunkan Cambel del Illes del counte de Fyf' (Duncan Campbell-of-the-Isles of the county of Fife) to 'Gregoire de Seint Cler' (Gregory Sinclair), we find a veritable roll-call of the leading families of Scotland

The vast majority of names on the Ragman Rolls are territorial or patronymics. There are just a tiny number of occupation names, for example Symon le Glover of Perth, Walter the Goldsmith of Roxburgh and Robert le Taillour of Stirling. There are no clear examples of nicknames.

THE NEXT GENERATION OF SCOTTISH SURNAMES

Once the concept of surnames was firmly established through the Anglo-Normans, the time was right for the establishment of more surnames.

Characteristic of Scotland is the freezing of the traditional patronymic system, thereby creating true surnames from them. The prefixes Mac and Mc (and even M') are no more than spelling variants. However, it has become conventional to apply one prefix or another to many surnames and for the convenience of our administrative systems it is now customary for bearers of such names to use one form or another. In indexes all three forms are taken together, and usually indexed separately from the letter M. These forms are now true surnames. MacDonald no longer means son of Donald; it is simply a surname. Macleod is not son of Leod, and conventionally dispenses with a capital for 'leod'.

Occupation names are something of a late developer in Scotland (in comparison with England) but they are reasonably common. Often the names of the occupations are different from those used in England, and therefore a little harder to recognize. Thus for example Lorimer is a harness maker, Brewster a brewer and Dempster an arbitrator, an officer in the Scottish courts (also found as Dempsie and Dempsey).

Scotland shows a marked process of anglicizing distinctive Scottish surnames. Following the Battle of Culloden (1746) and the defeat of Bonnie Prince Charlie, many Gaelic surnames were replaced by English forms. Often this was simply by translation from Gaelic to English, so MacIain became Johnson, MacLevy became Livingston and MacDonald became Donaldson or Donald. Sometimes the Mac– was dropped and the name stem spelt in the English way, so McGrimes became Graham.

The last three centuries have seen large-scale migration to Scotland from both England and Ireland. English surnames are well represented in Scotland. Kelly – an Irish surname – is the 39th most common surname in Scotland.

REGIONAL SURNAMES IN SCOTLAND

Scotland has many areas which are geographically remote, and this has favoured the development of surnames with a strong localization. Very many areas of Scotland could serve to illustrate. For example, the Isle of Bute has as its most common surname Kerr, a name of doubtful meaning but from the Old Norse language and reminding us that this island was once under Viking control. The fourth most common surname on Bute is Currie, a reduced form of MacVurich, itself from MacMuireach.

The Muireach who gave rise to this name can be identified: Muireach nicknamed Albannach (the Scot), an Irish poet of the 13th century who moved to the Isles.

SHETLAND

The one part of Scotland that has a completely different surname tradition from anywhere else in Scotland is Shetland (Orkney, by contrast, pretty much follows the Scots tradition). Shetland – the northernmost islands of Scotland – were for long part of Norway, and have a strong cultural identity with Norway. In early years Shetland simply used the Norse patronymic system, so Thorvald Thorreson (found in 1299) is simply Thorvald, Thor's son, and the patronymic would change in each generation. It is not a surname.

The most common ten surnames in Shetland (1804, from the *Meal Lists*) in order are: Anderson, Williamson, Robertson, Irvine, Smith, Tait, Jamieson, Johnson, Sinclair and Leask. These surnames are a mix of home-grown Shetland and imports. The five ending in –son are all Shetland home-grown (though they all evolved independently elsewhere). Curiously Johnson, in eighth position in 1804, is today's number one.

No Shetland place names appear to have become surnames in Shetland. Surnames such as Lerwick (from the largest town on Shetland) appear to have been adopted by families that moved away from Shetland. This is completely at odds with neighbouring Orkney, where many place names have engendered surnames. Shetland offers no apparent examples of occupational names which have become surnames, and no examples of nicknames. All home-grown Shetland surnames are therefore patronymics. Frequently they reflect the Norse first-name stock of the islands.

So Manson is from Magnus, and Hoseason from Hosea (a nickname from Osmund). Sometimes first names (from within the Viking, Norse tradition) are used as surnames without modification, as in Haakon and Eric.

Curiously Shetland has not only a different surname system but also a different first-name system. Norse first names have a long tradition on the island, while the Norman and Bible names found elsewhere in Scotland have been much less common. Middle names have been commonplace in Shetland from the early 18th century, more than a century before this became customary in Scotland.

TARTANS

Tartan has a strong association with Scottish surnames, with countless books claiming to link surnames with tartans. Most of these links are fiction.

Figure 16. In Scotland, surname, clan and tartan are strongly linked in popular culture, though in reality the connections are often more tenuous.

The process of weaving naturally leads to a check pattern. The very simplest is a check of black and white – effectively the two contrasting natural colours of sheep's wool – giving a striking tartan traditionally called the shepherd's plaid. It is but a step to add natural dyes to the warp and weft to create checks with greens, blues, reds, blacks and white, the colours most readily produced by vegetable dyes. Particular clans tended to favour particular patterns, but these patterns were subject to the whims of weavers (and their customers) and were certainly not formally set out.

Tartan under threat

All this was changed in the wake of Bonnie Prince Charlie's defeat at the Battle of Culloden (1746), when the government passed the Dress Act (1746), which banned tartan and banned the kilt. By such means the Highlanders were humiliated, prevented from wearing their everyday clothes and forced to adopt what to them were alien Lowland styles, including trousers. The Dress Act was repealed a generation later (1782), permitting Highlanders to wear again 'the Highland Dress which came down to the Clans from the beginning of the world'. But the damage had been done. Many of the patterns familiar in 1746 had simply been lost, while tartan as used in the years following 1782 was the dress of the poorest of Highlanders and granted little prestige.

History of tartans

What we today know about the traditional tartans of the Highlands 'from the beginning of the world' (or let's say from before 1746) comes broadly from three sources:

■ King George IV's visit to Edinburgh, 1822. This was the first time a king of Scotland had set foot in Scotland since 1641. He was fêted in Scotland with enormous nationalist pageantry, much of it choreographed by Sir Walter Scott. Tartan was suddenly in fashion, and for the first time in nearly a century the chieftains of the Highland clans appeared before the king in their family tartan, specially woven for the occasion. Possibly they did have an idea of the sort of tartan their great-grandfathers once wore. Possibly they made it up.

■ At the height of the excitement caused by George IV's visit, two brothers who said they were grandsons of Bonnie Prince Charlie claimed that they had an ancient manuscript giving details of tartans for the Highlands, Lowlands and Borders. This was exactly the information the upwardly mobile Scots wanted – especially in the Lowlands and Borders where there was very little tradition of tartan. Over the years they provided details piecemeal (so maximizing their revenue) leading to publication in 1842 of *Vestiarium Scoticum*, a book illustrating tartans and available at what was then a staggeringly high price of ten guineas. This book is now generally regarded as a fraud (and their claimed 'ancient manuscript' a myth) though it is likely that the brothers used actual patterns on those occasions when they were able to identify them.

■ Tartans created after *Vestiarium Scoticum* may use patterns associated with a particular area, but generally are simply new works of art.

All tartans sold today are considerably younger than the surnames they are linked with, and you can be almost sure that the tartan today associated with a name is not the same as that worn by the clan prior to 1746. Today no one should claim that they have a right to wear a particular tartan or that they are entitled to it;

rather they may simply chose to wear a particular tartan. Sometimes a clan association is active, and wearing a particular tartan as determined by the clan chief may be an outward sign of a link with a surname and a clan. The *Scottish Tartans Authority* has no authority to legislate on such matters, though it is an information source on tartan.

Is it Scots?

with best
wishes for
A. Merry Christmas
and A Happy New Year
from - Nan Campbell.

Figure 17. Robert Burns, Scotland's best-loved poet but with a surname from England's Cumbria.

Curiously many of the surnames we today associate with Scotland may in fact be English or Irish. There is no more Scottish-sounding name than Burns, today frequently encountered in Scotland and popularly associated with Scotland's national poet, Robbie Burns. Certainly the surname is naturalized in Scotland, but in origin should not be considered a Scottish name. The surname appears to have just one early source – from which most Burns derive their line. The name is a place name in origin, but not a Scottish one. It derives from Burnesshead in Cumberland, and early spellings of the surname include Burness and Bernes. Today the surname is most frequently encountered in South West Scotland, particularly Ayrshire, the home of Robbie Burns. The 17th century plantation of Ulster took the name to Ireland, and it is well represented there too. In its original English homeland the name is less common.

ACTIVITY

Exploring the Ragman Rolls

This fundamental document for Scottish surname history is readily available online. An easy source is Rampant Scotland at **www.rampant scotland.com/ragman/blragman_index.htm**

This site has made the blunder of transcribing an orthographic form of non-final –s as if it is –f, leading to such errors as 'prioriffa' for *prorissa* (prioress) and 'Aberdonenfis' for *Aberdonensis* (Aberdeenshire). With this caution made, it is a super presentation of two great Scottish documents and a name list which it is possible to browse at length. The names are in alphabetical order, so even when the spelling on the Ragman Roll is idiosyncratic, finding a particular name shouldn't be too problematic.

With a few exceptions Scottish surnames in Mc–/Mac– are not on the Ragman Roll, but very many of the remainder are. For many Scottish surnames this is their first recording, and in many cases must be the first man to bear the surname. This is a document at the start of Scottish surname history.

ACTIVITY

Scotland's People

The Scotland's People website (**www.scotlandspeople.gov.uk**) offers about 80 million records and is a primary source for Scottish history and genealogy. On its entry page it has a 'Free Surname Search'. It is as simple as entering the surname you are interested in and seeing what is available.

17

Irish Surnames

Irish surnames show evidence of three great influences.

- The earliest is the Celtic name stock which contributes the majority of Irish surnames.

- The Anglo-Norman invasion of Ireland brought Norman names to Ireland.

- The plantation of Ulster and the development of Dublin as the second city of the British Empire brought Scottish and English names to Ireland.

Additionally there are minor influences in Irish surname practice. That of the Viking settlement of Dublin is an intriguing case needing more investigation. Huguenot influence is shown by surnames such as Lefaun, while a handful of continental surnames witness trade between Irish ports and the continent. Among these, Switzer has become established.

CELTIC IRISH NAMES

Celtic surnames from Ireland are claimed to include some of the oldest from the British Isles. Certainly there are some old Irish surnames, though the position is not as simple as may be thought. For example, the oft-repeated claim that 10th-century High King Brian Boru required the Irish to take surnames appears apocryphal; Irish surnames are early but not quite that early.

The tradition of identifying someone as the son of their father is a mainstay of the Celtic naming tradition in Ireland, Scotland, Wales and elsewhere. Ireland makes extensive use of the prefix O', meaning grandson, descendant or kin, a custom which was not adopted in Scotland. Additionally Ireland makes some use of the prefix Mac–/Mc–, a custom that was carried to Scotland with the medieval migration of the Irish tribe the Scots from Ireland to what came to be called Scotland.

Among the earliest of Irish surnames is O'Brien, descendant of Brian, usually interpreted as meaning the descendants of Brian Boru the High King of Ireland. It seems that early bearers of this name were keen to claim Brian Boru as their ancestor and it is possible that they were right in so doing, but the name would have been adopted several generations later than Brian Boru. O'Brien may plausibly be a late 11th-century surname, but Brian Boru lived more than a century earlier, in the late 10th century. Rather the surname implies membership of the kin of Brian Boru, and therefore membership of the clan that provided Ireland with four high kings and around thirty kings of Thomond (North Munster) as well as the line of the extant Baron Inchiquin – a proud tradition indeed.

Many Irish surnames refer not to clan but to a *sept* – a sub-group within a clan – to which the progenitor belonged. In Irish such names end in –ain, as in O'Suileabhain. Anglicized, this becomes a surname in –an, Sullivan. The –an ending is commonplace in Ireland producing such names as Regan, Callaghan, Donovan, Ryan and Nolan. Such names testify to origin at a time when the clan system was still active, which in Ireland suggests formation prior to 1541, the date of the formal establishment of the Kingdom of Ireland.

A peculiarity of Irish naming is that the prefixes Mac–, Mc– and O′ have at various times been seen as little more than formal versions of a surname which may also be spoken and written without that prefix. This contrasts with the Scottish system where the prefix Mac– or Mc– is fixed to the surname. Someone with the surname Niall might be addressed by this name for everyday purposes but for formal use insist on O′Niall. The prefix is used almost as the titles Mr and Mrs were used in England in a more formal age, and like these titles it doesn't change the surname. Within an Irish context Niall and O′Niall should be regarded simply as the same name.

HIBERNO-NORMAN NAMES

The 12th-century Anglo-Norman settlement of Ireland brought many Anglo-Norman surnames to Ireland. In Ireland the Anglo-Normans encountered a pre-existing surname system (in contrast with Scotland and Wales where the systems were purely patronymic).

Some Anglo-Norman surnames have become in effect character-istic Irish names. Fitzgerald, Butler, and Burke are examples. The Irish patronymic-derived surnames flourished alongside the Anglo-Norman imports. A few families actually used two surnames. So for example the family of Peter de Bermingham used both the Anglo-Norman Birmingham and an Irish patrony-mic based on Peter – MacFeeter.

ANGLICIZATION OF IRISH NAMES

Much of the recording of Irish names over the centuries has been by English-speaking officials, most of whom had no knowledge of the Irish language. In most cases they wrote what they thought they heard, and in many cases Celtic Irish names were progressively anglicized. Erratic spellings are a prominent feature of Irish surnames. Today many people, particularly in the Irish Republic, are returning their names to an Irish-language spelling, or correcting some of the excesses of English spelling. In many cases the prefix Mac–/Mc– or O' is being re-adopted where it is seen as traditional.

English pressure to adopt an English surname was intense. In 1465 a law (applied in Counties Dublin, Meath, Louth and Kildare) required Irish people to adopt English surnames, specifying 'an English surname of a town as Sutton, Chester, Trim, Skreen, Cork, Kinsale; or a colour as White, Black, Brown; or an art as Smith or Carpenter; or an office as Cook or Butler'. The law did not appear to accept patronymics, and seems specifically intended to discourage the Irish patronymic practice. In such cases the adoption of surnames would seem to be largely arbitrary, and in many cases subsequent reversion to Irish surnames is likely.

PLANTATION NAMES

The early 17th-century Plantation of Ulster brought Scottish families and Scottish names to Ireland's northern province – as well as to Dublin and some parts of the south of Ireland. Even today these names tend to be associated with the Protestant faith, and with Unionist politics.

Associated with Ulster are the surnames of the Lowland Scots, particularly the south-eastern counties of Galloway, Kirkcud-brightshire, Dumfriesshire and Ayrshire. There is strong representation from the Scottish border, particularly of the 'reiver' families – that dominated the area: Armstrong, Elliott, Irvine, Johnston, Nixon.

While some 'Macs' in Ireland are undoubtedly home-grown products of the Irish system, many and probably the majority of Irish Macs are in origin migrants from Scotland.

Viking names

An area which needs more investigation is that of Viking surnames in Irish. The story has the potential to be an exciting development in perceptions of Irish history, and is worth at least a note here.

The Viking rule of Dublin ended in 1171, a date by which some surnames certainly existed. Indeed the Irish king who conquered Dublin had a surname – King Dermot MacMurrough of Leinster. It has been suggested that a handful of Irish surnames – of which Doyle is the outstanding example – bear witness to Viking ancestors. Doyle (and MacDougall, MacDowell) is from the Irish *Dubhghoill* meaning 'dark foreigner'. We should probably understand 'dark' to mean threatening, and used as a boast. Linguistically this origin is probable. The distribution of the surname corresponds with areas of Viking settlement – centred on County Dublin, but also found in Counties Wexford, Wicklow, Carlow, Kerry and Cork, all Viking areas. However, Y-chromosome analysis of people living in County Dublin has failed to find any genetic heritage whatsoever from the Norwegian Vikings who ruled there. We are left with an unresolved question. If the geneticists are right that the Viking genetic heritage of Dublin (and Ireland) is effectively zero, then there are no patrilinear lines going back to the Vikings, and therefore no Viking surnames. My own view is that there is a problem with the geneticists' identification of a particular Y-chromosome with the Norwegian Vikings (both in Ireland and everywhere else). Rather I think the evidence of history is that the Norwegian Vikings should be identical to the Danish Vikings – and we already know the Danish Vikings were identical to the Anglo-Saxons. As Ireland is awash with what we usually identify as Anglo-Saxon genes, there is on the basis of this argument no problem with apparently lacking Viking genes.

A list of Irish surnames which may plausibly come to be identified as Viking in origin (following E. MacLysaght, *Irish Families: Their Names, Arms and Origins*, 1985) is: Arthur, Beirne, Bligh, Boland, Caskey, Coll, Coppinger, Doyle, Gohery, Hanrick (and Hendrick), Harold, Higgins, Kells, Kettle, Loughlin (and McLoughlin), McGetrick, Nelson, Norris, O'Higgins, Sugrue, Sweetnam, Thunder (and Toner) and Tormey.

IRISH REGIONALISM

Very many Irish surnames show strong county patterns. This indicates both a lack of movement of populations within Ireland – less than seems to have been the case elsewhere in the British Isles for example – and also argue for a relatively late date of formation of many of the names. While Ireland certainly includes some of the earliest British Isles surnames as well as some Anglo-Norman surnames, names of this age are unusual – most Irish surnames are more recent, many from the 16th and 17th centuries.

The regional distribution is indicated by comparing the neighbouring counties of Antrim and Derry/Londonderry. The most common five surnames in County Antrim are Smith, Johnston,

Stewart, Wilson and Thompson, all originating outside of Ireland. Indeed, a majority of the surnames from County Antrim are Lowland Scottish and reflect the 17th-century plantation of much of the county by settlers from Lowland Scotland. However, across the River Bann in County Derry/Londonderry the surname pattern is completely different. Here the most common five names are O'Doherty, McLaughlin, Kelly, Bradley and Brown, with the first three being clear Irish names. Indeed O'Doherty and McLaughlin are both characteristic County Donegal names and seem to reflect the movement of 19th-century migrants from rural County Donegal into the fast-growing city of Derry/Londonderry. The most common surnames of these two Ulster counties show no overlap with many of the counties elsewhere in Ireland. For example, in County Limerick the most common five names are Ryan, O'Brien, Fitzgerald, Sullivan and Hayes. The point may be repeated county by county – Ireland demonstrates an extreme regionalization of surnames.

Sometimes the regionalization is more specific even than a county. O'Shaughnessy is specific not to the whole county but just to the south of County Galway, an area nicknamed as early as 1585 'O'Shaughnessy's country'. The name appears in the multiplicity of forms characteristic of Irish surnames, including the Irish Gaelic spelling O'Seachnasaigh, and the anglicized variants Shornessy, Shawnessy and Shaughnessy.

IRISH SURNAMES TODAY

The Republic of Ireland has two official languages – Irish and English – the teaching of both of which is compulsory in schools. Place names and personal names all have forms in both languages. Thus for example the name of the country is in

English (*Republic of Ireland*) and in Irish (*Éire*), while the place known in English as *Dingle* is in Irish *An Daingean*. When speaking or writing in Irish it is usual to use the Modern Irish forms of names. The president of Ireland, at the time of publication, Mary Patricia McAleese, is in Irish Máire Pádraigín Bean Mhic Ghiolla Íosa. Today all Irish surnames have forms in both the English and Irish languages. The top ten surnames of the Irish Republic are as follows.

1.	Murphy	Ó Murchú
2.	Kelly	Ó Ceallaigh
3.	O'Sullivan	Ó Súilleabháin
4.	Walsh	Breathnach
5.	Smith	Mac Gabhann
6.	O'Brien	Uí Bhriain
7.	Byrne	Ó Broin
8.	Ryan	Ó Riain
9.	O'Connor	Ó Conchobhair
10.	O'Neill	Ó Néill

Such forms refect variously differences in Irish orthography (Ó Néill as the Irish spelling of an identical English form O'Neill); the Irish convention of putting Ó before most names (so English Murphy but Irish Ó Murchú); the Irish phonological process of changing Ó to Uí before certain sounds (so English O'Brien but Irish Uí Bhriain); and translation (so Smith to Mac Gabhann, strictly 'son of the smith'). The etymology of Walsh ('foreigner') has been reflected in the translation Breathnach ('Briton'). Additionally the process has led to the use of hybrid English-Irish forms. Thus O'Byrne is occasionally found as a variant of Byrne. Also encountered is the adoption not of Modern Irish forms but of Old Irish forms – for example Ryan becomes Ó Riagháin.

ACTIVITY

The homes of Irish surnames

A key source for Irish surnames is Griffith's *Valuation of Ireland*, a survey of land and property taken 1846–1865 which names all landowners and tenants. It therefore includes virtually all Irish families for the period and shows where in Ireland they were living. It was not originally indexed; however, a *General Index of Surnames* is now available (county-by-county, typewritten and on microfiche) through major libraries, including the British Library (London), National Library of Ireland (Dublin), National Archives of Ireland (Dublin), Public Record Office of Northern Ireland (Belfast), and some local library and record centres. Using this document it is possible to see the distribution of surnames in the mid-19th century and so localize an Irish surname.

ACTIVITY

A visit to the National Archives of Ireland

The National Archives of Ireland are the repository of the largest collection of documentary material on the history of Ireland, including much that is relevant for surname study. Most of the first records of Irish surnames are in their collection.

Sources available online include the 1901 and 1911 census returns. These are key genealogical documents for Ireland. The indexes can be used to indicate the distribution of surnames at these dates and therefore help to identify surname homes. The 1901 census was taken by census enumerators who frequently wrote down surnames as they heard them or with the spelling they considered established. However, the 1911 census was written out by a member of each household – in theory by the head of the household though in practice often by another member who had a greater level of literacy. The 1911 census therefore records surnames as the families themselves thought they should be spelt. Comparison of 1901 and 1911 census returns may indicate different spellings.

ACTIVITY

Irish culture and language

Surnames of Ireland are a tangible link with the history and culture of Ireland. The 19th-century Irish diaspora has transported these surnames around the then British Empire, particularly to England and the USA. An interest in an Irish surname may well be an opening both for Irish and those of Irish descent into the history of Ireland. The very earliest Irish surnames evoke the Irish heroic age, while all bear witness to events in the turbulent history of Ireland. A visit to the National Museum of Ireland (Dublin) and the many regional museums and heritage centres of Ireland is a great way to appreciate this history.

Remember that most Irish surnames are names in the Irish Gaelic language, and their spelling and pronunciation in English usually differ from the Irish original. The best possible appreciation of such surnames comes through knowledge of the Irish language.

18

Isle of Man Surnames

Situated in the middle of the Irish Sea, the Isle of Man has had, as a consequence of its location, a distinctive history and a distinctive pattern of surname development. From at least the 5th century the island was inhabited by the Scots – the tribe then living in Ireland and which had not yet migrated to Scotland. These Celtic-speaking Scots are the dominant ethnicity and culture of the Isle of Man, with their Celtic Manx language enduring until the mid-20th century, and even undergoing a modest revival today. From the 9th century the Isle of Man was governed by the Dublin Vikings who introduced some Norse first names – as well as starting the Isle of Man parliament, the world's earliest continuous parliament extant today. The Isle of Man passed into Scots rule in 1266, and after several vacillations into English rule. Today the Isle of Man is a British Crown Dependency, neither a part of the United Kingdom nor of the European Union.

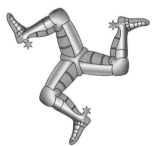

Figure 18. The strange emblem of the Isle of Man reminds us that it is a place apart, as do its unique surnames.

The history of Isle of Man surnames is a strange one. By the early 16th century the prefix Mac– was almost universal for surnames on the Isle of Man. By the early 17th century it had all but vanished. This striking linguistic development dominates the surnames scene of the Isle of Man.

The Mac prefix

The prefix Mac– is unstressed in the Manx language, as it is in the related Celtic languages Irish and Scots Gaelic. Where syllables are unstressed there is always the possibility of them being further reduced, so the concept of a surname in Mac– losing this prefix is not wholly unexpected. Yet with a very few exceptions it has not happened in Ireland or in Scotland. The unique feature in the Isle of Man is the ubiquitous usage of this prefix by the early 16th century. Plausibly the prefix had gone beyond its original meaning 'son of' and become a polite opening, comparable to the traditional English placing of 'mister' before any man's surname as a term of respect. Once the prefix Mac– was truly universal it was also all but meaningless. Just as the English 'mister' is in modern usage increasingly omitted, so Mac– stopped being used.

On the Isle of Man the reduction of Mac– was not to nothing at all but rather to its final consonant, –k–, which was tagged on to the start of the surname. So MacCathain became Caine, MacAedha became Kay, MacDermot became Kermode and MacCuinn became Quine. Where once almost all Isle of Man surnames had commenced with Mac–, now they commenced with a –k– sound variously spelt C, K and QU. Frequently the change in the initial sound encouraged mutations further on in the name, so the transformations which occurred in the 16th century were profound, and produced a set of names unlike those of elsewhere in the British Isles.

Popular Isle of Man surnames

The 1881 census shows the top ten surnames of the Isle of Man as Kelly, Quayle, Caine, Corlett, Christian, Clague, Moore, Faragher,

Cannell, Quirk. These names are strikingly different from the name stock elsewhere in the British Isles. With the exception of Kelly and Moore (both common in Ireland), these names would be considered unusual anywhere else in the British Isles.

Occupational names derive from the Manx language (and are therefore hard for people who don't speak Manx to spot). Examples include Brew (farmer), Clague (leech or doctor), Crye (weaver), Monier (steward) and Vondy (yeoman).

The rule of the Lancashire Stanley family over the Isle of Man in the 15th, 16th and 17th centuries has led to a circumstance where many Lancashire place names have given rise to Isle of Man surnames, including Bootle, Heysham, Holland (from Up Holland), Prescott and Standish.

ACTIVITY

Exploring Isle of Man surnames
There is plenty of material available.

▶ Key books include the following. Moore is effectively the founder of Manx surname studies and cannot be missed. Kneen is perhaps too centred on Irish names. Gill was published in 1963 but in fact was written in the 1930s, so it is older than it looks. Quilliam (a good Manx surname) is reasonably recent and accessible.
A. W. Moore, *The Surnames and Place-names of the Isle of Man*, London, Elliot Stock, 1890 (also 2nd revised edition 1906).
J. J. Kneen, *Personal Names of the Isle of Man*, Oxford, Oxford University Press, 1937.
W. W. Gill, *Third Manx Scrapbook*, London, Arrowsmith, 1963.
L. Quilliam, *Surnames of the Manks*, Cashtal Books, 1989.

▶ Online a great starting point is the Manx National Heritage website at **www.gov.im/mnh/**

19

Channel Island Surnames

The Channel Islands have long been attached to the English crown, but their language has until recently been Norman French and their culture and surname practices often French rather than English. The Channel Islands include some of the earliest British Isles surnames, names such as Brehault (Guernsey) and De Gruchy (Jersey). At the time of the Norman Conquest the Channel Islands were part of the Duchy of Normandy (a position they retain). In effect they should be regarded for surname purposes as part of Normandy. They are certainly part of the Norman adoption of surnames from the early 11th century. Subsequently the language has been French, and home-grown Channel Island surnames are French-language surnames. Thus for example the French definite article is found in Le Page, Le Prevost and Le Sauvage, which are all surnames from Guernsey.

The two main islands of Jersey and Guernsey each have surnames distinctive of the particular island. Some have remained on the one island, but there are also examples of surnames which first became established on one island and then spread to the other. Additionally there are English surnames which have become naturalised in the Channel Islands.

Guernsey.

GUERNSEY BANKING COMPANY.

The chief business of this Company, is to draw and cash Bills on London and Paris, to discount Promissory Notes, and to advance money.

The Bank is open every day, (Sundays and Holidays excepted) from ten o'clock in the morning, till three in the afternoon, at Mrs. Bodilly's house, High-street.

AGENTS TO THE FIRE AND LIFE ASSURANCE COMPANIES.

Atlas, F. C. Lukis, High-street.
Alliance, John Bonamy, Grange-road.
London Assurance Corporation, W. H. Brock, Ann's-place.
Eagle Life-office, J. Weaver, Office, High-Street.
Norwich Union, Matthew Barbet, High-Street.
Phœnix, William Solbé Sheppard, High-Street.
Royal Exchange, John Mellish, High-Street.
Royal, of France, Harry Dobrée, High-Street.
Sun, James Barbet, Jun. at Advocate Jeremie's office.
Union, James Arnold, High-street.
West of England, Peter Solbé, Cordiers.
County Fire office and } Wm. Maillard, Mansell-street.
Provident Life office, }

STATES' OFFICERS.

James Du Port, Assistant Supervisor.   Office at No. 203, Pollet-street.
John De Carteret, Harbour Master of St. Peter-Port.
Alexander Deschamps, Deputy Harbour Master, ditto.
Office at Mrs. Belin's, Pollet-street.
David Macculloch, Receiver of the States Dues on Spirituous Liquors.   Office in Pollet-street.
Mr. M. P. Goodwin, Surveyor of the Roads and Public Works, Paris-street.

St. SAMPSON'S HARBOUR.

Eleazar Le Marchant, esq. Supervisor of the Harbour.
R. W. Isemonger, Master of ditto.
Henry Rouget, Deputy-Master of ditto.

AGENT FOR LLOYD'S.—Anthony Isemonger, Smith-st.

Guernsey.

CONSTABLES OF ALL THE PARISHES.

St. PETER-PORT.

HIGH-CONSTABLES.

Ed. Collings, Bordage-st. | Peter Martel, Canichers.

ASSISTANT - CONSTABLES.

Wm. Bronard, Glatney, | John Aptor, High-street,
A. Le Mesurier, Burnt-lane, | John Snow, Haute-Ville.

James Frecker, Market-Constable.

St. SAMPSON...John Ogier, jun. and Michael Collas.
VALE.........Francis Allez and Nicholas Mahy.
CATEL.......Dan. Le Messurier and Js.-B. Moullin.
St. SAVIOUR..James Alexandre and Peter Mansell.
FOREST......Peter Mauger and George Torode.
TORTEVAL.....Wm. Simon and John Robilliard.
St. PETER....Peter D. Simon and John Langlois.
St. MARTIN...John De Putron and Henry Mauger.
St. ANDREW..John Blondel and William Lihou.

TOWN HOSPITAL.

JOHN VALRENT, Treasurer.
ELIAS GUERIN, Vice-Treasurer.

DIRECTORS.

Daniel Le Masurier, | Andrew J. Naftel,
Peter Bienvenu, | Francis De Putron,
Elias Mourant, | Peter Le Lievre.

COLLECTORS.

John De Putron | John De Jersey,
John Bertram, | James Mourant,
John D. G. Touzeau, | Daniel G. Le Masurier.

SAVINGS BANK.

On the 31st December 1829, there were 944 Depositors. Deposits may amount to £15 in the first year, and £10 each succeeding year until the principal amounts to £100.—Amount of Deposits lent to the States £20,000. Attendance on Saturdays from 11 till 1 o'clock.—Interest paid on the first and second Saturdays in January and July.

Figure 19. The distinctive form of Guernsey surnames is indicated by this 1830 directory.

Figure 20. The miles of sea separating the main islands of the Channel Islands ensured that distinctive surnames evolved on each island.

ACTIVITY

Exploring the Channel Islands

▶ There is specialist material both in the libraries of the Channel Islands, in the major libraries of the British Isles, as well as some on the internet.

▶ For Jersey a good starting point is 'Some Jersey surnames: Their origin and meaning' in *Annual Bulletin*, Société Jersiaise, XIV, part 1.

▶ To get started with Guernsey surnames try the Guernsey Surname Resource Centre at **www.surnameweb.org/Guernsey/surnames.htm**

20

Understanding Jewish Surnames of the British Isles

Jewish surnames are a long-established part of the British Isles surname stock. While there were very small numbers of Jewish people in medieval England, the first big migration was around 1500. Jewish surnames in the British Isles therefore have a history of just over five centuries.

THE SEPHARDIM

In 1492 – the year Columbus voyaged to America – the Spanish monarchs King Ferdinand and Queen Isabella required that everyone living in their kingdoms should either adopt Christianity or leave. The policy was extended to Portugal in the following year. It took a few years to take effect, but its impact was profound. Iberia had large Muslim and Jewish communities, established there for centuries, and it was these faiths that Ferdinand and Isabella aimed to eradicate. Many of both faiths simply converted and became assimilated within Christian Spain; very many emigrated. Muslims largely fled to North Africa; Jews were widely spread within Europe. Numbers are enormous – about 750,000 Jews fled from Spain and Portugal at this time.

The Jews who arrived in Britain around 1500 were mainly from Portugal and for some generations spoke both their community language of Ladino and English. Most were notionally recorded as Christian, as England at this time did not officially allow Judaism, yet in practice their Jewish faith was tolerated. Their community – the Sephardic Jews or Sephardim – flourished in London.

Some of these Sephardic Jews had patronymic names in the Hebrew fashion. Thus David ben Joseph is David the son of Joseph, and Miriam bat Aaron is Miriam the daughter of Aaron. These patronymics readily became fixed and the patronymic marker – *ben* or *bat* – simply dropped. But most of the community already had surnames formed according to the principles of Portuguese surname usage – names such as Da Costa, Disraeli, Lindo, Mocatta, and Montefiore, names which have become established in the British Isles, though are still unusual. Others adopted surnames from the British Isles stock or modified their surnames to conform to the conventions of surnames in London. Thus David becomes Davis.

These Sephardic families had a substantial numerical impact on the population of London, some remaining Jewish through the centuries, many converting to Christianity. Best known of the London Sephardim is Victorian Prime Minister Benjamin Disraeli, himself a Christian, but from Jewish ancestry.

THE ASHKENAZIM

A second and larger migration of Jewish people to the British Isles was in the 19th century, particularly following the uncertainty of the 1848 'Year of Revolutions' in Europe. These were the Ashkenazi Jews or Ashkenazim, mostly from Germany, Poland,

Figure 21. London's Great Synagogue bears witness to an historic Jewish community in London which contributed many English surnames.

Lithuania, Ukraine, White Russia and Great Russia. Most spoke Yiddish – a mixed language of German, Hebrew and various Slavic languages – and many continued to speak Yiddish alongside English after their arrival in the British Isles. Some had surnames in the German system, and many apparently German surnames in the British Isles are better regarded as surnames of the Ashkenazim. However, those from lands further east where Slavic languages predominated came from cultures where the poor used patronymics rather than surnames – in contrast with the rich, who used both patronymics and surnames, the practice which has become standard in Russia today. Jews in these countries were usually the poor and therefore usually had no surnames, and a consequence is that (remarkably) many of the Ashkenazim who migrated to the British Isles just a century and a half ago had no surname. The surnames were adopted after arrival in the British Isles.

Many Ashkenazim identified with one of the traditional three-fold divisions of the Jewish people: Kohein, Levites and Israelites. These names gave three surnames: Cohen, Levy and Israel, names which may be regarded as characteristic of the Ashkenazim (beware however, Cohan, which is usually an Irish surname). The Ashkenazim often used patronymics, and metronymic names are reasonably frequently encountered: Reises and Rifkind are both examples.

ACTIVITY

Investigating Jewish surnames
The key to investigating a British Isles Jewish surname is to decide what sort of Jewish surname it is.

▶ Is the name Sephardi or Ashkenazi? If Ashkenazi, is it German or Slavic?

▶ If Sephardi, the name almost certainly relates to families established in London for around five centuries. There is an established body of London Sephardim names, both the original Portuguese names, and a number of patronymics based on the names of Old Testament figures: Joseph, David (and Davis), Moses (and Moss) and Solomon. Genealogical research may in theory take a line back as far as the Sephardim migration of five centuries ago and therefore the ultimate British Isles origin of the name. Some records do exist, both those of the Bevis Marks synagogue in London and the mass of London records, though the task of tracing a line is challenging.

▶ If Ashkenazi and German in origin, the surname is likely to have a single originator, probably a migrant to the British Isles in the middle of the 19th century. Thus Bensburg derives from a single migrant of around 1850, Caspar Bensburg. As most migrants in this wave were relatively young when they came to Britain (almost all under 34), an Ashkenazi German surname suggests an ancestor born in Germany sometime between the Battle of Waterloo which ended the Napoleonic wars (1815) and 1850. If you are investigating an Ashkenazi name you have every chance of finding the single British Isles progenitor. All who have this name today will probably be related. Such names are particularly satisfying as they provide the possibility of drawing up a tree which includes every single bearer of the surname.

▶ German names have often been modified, for example Hertz to Harris. Often the modification is within the last century and reflects the legacy of two world wars when living in the British Isles and bearing an apparently German surname was undesirable. Some families have reverted their name to its German original.

▶ Names created in the British Isles by Slavic Ashkenazim are some of the most changeable surnames. Many are better regarded as patronymics or by-names, and children do not necessarily have the same surnames as their fathers. Families did not feel any particular sense of ownership of the surname they adopted. As with the Sephardim, the Ashkenazim adopted many Old Testament first names, with the result that such patronymic-derived surnames cannot be known with certainty to be Sephardi or Ashkenazi.

▶ Cohen, Levy and Israel are characteristic Ashkenazim names. Cohen is the name of the Jewish hereditary priesthood and claims descent from Aaron, brother of Moses.

▶ A very few Slavic surnames were brought to the British Isles by the Sephardim.

ACTIVITY

Jewish geneaology

The topic is enormous and in parts highly specialized, yet much can nonetheless be accessed by non-specialists. Copious information is available on those surnames which are Jewish. Key websites are the following.

Jewish Genealogical Society of Great Britain, **www.jgsgb.org.uk**
JewishGen, **www.jewishgen.org**
Sephardic Studies, **www.sephardicstudies.org**

21

Identifying Gypsy Surnames of the British Isles

The Romany Gypsies have a history of a millennium-long migration from the Indian subcontinent. Quite who they were in India and why they started to move is still a matter for debate. The broad outline of their westward migration is now established – through Persia and Asia Minor, across the Bosphorus into Europe, and through the Balkans and Central Europe to all parts of the continent. The first record of Romany Gypsies in the British Isles is 1506 (in Scotland). As the migrants believed they came from Egypt (and perhaps some did pass through Egypt), they were called Egyptians or Gypsies. In an early example of ethnic intolerance they were banned from England by King Henry VIII (1530). A generation later they were granted the right to stay by Mary I (1554) on condition that they set aside 'naughty, idle and ungodly life and company'. The requirement was in effect that they should conform to the norms of English society, and, to the English administrators who had to confirm that they were doing this, that included the use of surnames.

GYPSIES TAKE SURNAMES

The Romany Gypsies who came to the British Isles from the early 16th century came with their own language – Romany, an Indian language – and with a distinct culture and ethnicity. Romany Gypsy lifestyle in the British Isles was at first nomadic and later semi-nomadic. Settled life came late – mostly in the late 19th and early 20th centuries, with almost all adopting a settled lifestyle by the 1950s. Thus the Romany Gypsies in the British Isles have now almost all abandoned their traditional way of life, and for their descendants the surnames are one of the few relics of their Romany Gypsy culture.

Figure 22. These London Gypsies of the turn of the 19th century had their own culture, language and surnames.

Gypsy surnames are not wholly a product of life in the British Isles, for a handful of surnames appear to have been brought to the British Isles by early Gypsy migrants. However, the vast majority have been adopted subsequently. Gypsy surnames fall into several categories.

▪ Surnames within the Romany Gypsy language, for example Petulengro.

▪ Translations of surnames from Romany to English, so Petulengro becomes Smith. The surname is particularly appropriate as many Gypsies were itinerant smiths.

▪ Adoption of a 'prestige' non-Gypsy surname, for example the surname of a patron on whose lands gypsies have lived, or simply that of a well-known family. Gray, Lovell and Stanley are examples.

▪ Adoption of a 'common' non-Gypsy surname so as to be inconspicuous. Smith and Brown seem especially to have been favoured.

▪ Inter-marriage with a non-Gypsy family leading to adoption of that family's surname, even in cases where it was the mother who was the non-Gypsy.

The most common surnames used by gypsies are Lee, Heron (or Herne), Smith, Gray, Boswell, Taylor and Young. All of these surnames may be borne by non-Gypsies, though Boswell is rare outside of families of Gypsy origin. Gypsies often favoured unusual first names, including many obscure and resounding names from the Old Testament, in part as a counterbalance to surnames which were common within the Gypsy community. Zechariah Lee and Urania Boswell – the early 20th century king and queen of the Gypsies – are examples of full British Isles Gypsy names.

GYPSY VIEWS ON SURNAMES

In many Gypsy families the surname was seen largely as a name of convenience for dealing with administration and non-Gypsy families. Sometimes surnames were transmitted from mother to children (even when the parents were married), reflecting the matrilinear conventions of Gypsy society. Very many Gypsy families routinely used two or more surnames, one for use within their own community and one for use with non-Gypsies. Thus Chumomisto might be translated Boswell, both meaning 'kiss-well' – the English slang word *to bos* which means *to kiss* is now largely forgotten but once commonplace. Similarly Purrun meaning an onion might be translated, though the translation chosen is 'leek', usually shortened to Lee. Many Gypsies pronounce this surname with a slight aspiration at the end (like the *ch* in Scottish *loch*), encouraging the spelling variant Leigh.

Figure 23. These early 20th-century Scottish Gypsies shared surnames with Gypsy families both throughout the British Isles and in the British Empire and the USA.

Gypsies have the concept of a tribe as a group of interrelated families. Sometimes these are geographically defined, as the 'Tribe of Epping Forest'; often they are expressed in terms of descent from an ancestor, who is usually described by a first name, as 'Tribe of Moses'. These tribal identities seemingly had more meaning to Gypsies than surnames did. Tribes and surnames sometimes overlapped. Some of the biggest Gypsy families had the concept of in-marriage, whereby the convention was to restrict choice of partners to someone of the same tribe, which often meant a cousin with the same surname. Brian Vesey-Fitzgerald, an early Gypsy scholar, reports being told 'Lees recordin' to rights should marry with Lees' and the rule does seem to have been kept to until well into the 19th century.

Gypsy society also had the concept of gypsy kings and queens – effectively the leaders of tribes or larger groups who would handle interaction with non-Gypsies. Selection appears to have been by a process partly hereditary, partly by acclamation. Surnames could be adopted to stress relationship with the relative from whom the honour was being inherited.

TINKERS

Tinkers are not Romany Gypsies, but they are often called Gypsies. Their lifestyle in many ways resembled that of the Romany Gypsies, and they were frequently subject to the same laws. Additionally they first came to England about the same time as the Romany Gypsies, making confusion of the two groups by the English population that much easier. Tinkers take their name from their most common occupation, that of tinker or itinerant pot mender.

Though now found throughout the British Isles, Tinkers are Irish in origin. They are a group that for centuries lived alongside the Irish in Ireland, maintaining their own distinct language (Shelta) and a semi-nomadic culture. They are sometimes called Irish Travellers. Mostly, they use surnames from the Irish surname stock. There do not appear to be any Irish surnames which are uniquely Tinker, but there are surnames which are especially common among this group. These include (in a rough order of their frequency) Driscoll, Sullivan, Sheridan, Coffey, Quilligan, Flynn, Leary and Donoghue.

The surname Tinker and its variant Tinkler is an English occupational name – meaning a mender of pots – and appears to have arisen in England in the 13th century, first recorded in Somerset in 1243 (in *The Assize Rolls of Somerset*). It is by no means certain that the first bearer of this name was a member of the ethnic group the Tinkers, or that any bearer of the surname Tinker is a descendant of the Tinkers. Rather the surname is older than the application of the occupational name to the ethnic group.

APPROACHING GYPSY SURNAMES

This is one of the most emotive areas of family tree research. Very many Romany Gypsy families who settled a century ago brought up their children as non-Gypsies and as a consequence the knowledge of Gypsy roots has often been lost. Similarly, Tinker families have often identified as Irish rather than Tinker, and their distinctive heritage often forgotten. The concept that Boswell is most probably Romany Gypsy or Leary most probably Tinker may not be welcome.

An alternative view is that of the Victorian romanticism of the

Gypsy way of life, which appears to offer an exciting alternative to more conventional lifestyles. Today the negative perceptions of the Romany Gypsies and Tinkers, particularly as it developed in the first half of the 20th century, is largely forgotten, and it is perhaps easier to take pride in Gypsy roots.

Many Gypsies worked in the late-Victorian travelling circuses, adding an element of colour and adventure to a family tree. And yes, the lifestyle caused surname change. Many performers had colourful stage names, and these invented names could be adopted as surnames.

ACTIVITY

Identifying Gypsy surnames

▶ It is very hard to identify a Romany Gypsy surname in isolation. Lee may be Gypsy, or may be English. Gray may be a Gypsy family, or may be a long-established family of English aristocrats. But clusters of surnames within a family are informative. A family whose members are called Lee, Heron and Gray is almost certainly Romany Gypsy.

▶ Identifying Tinker surnames is even harder. Indeed it is unlikely that the surnames alone would be enough to make an identification. A mix of Romany Gypsy surnames and (apparently) Irish surnames within a family may indicate Tinker roots, reflecting the frequent inter-marriage of Romany Gypsies and Tinkers in the late 19th and early 20th centuries.

▶ Occupations are often a key to Gypsy ethnicity, and jobs such as hawker and horse dealer found alongside a possible Gypsy surname is suggestive.

▶ Pronunciation can be durable. Lee with a final aspiration perhaps with recent interchange with the spelling Leigh suggests the Gypsy name. Heron often has its second syllable clipped, as 'her-n', giving an alternative spelling as Hern.

▶ The whole name is often the key to identifying a Gypsy surname, as Gypsies have traditionally been adventurous in their choice of names. Unusual Old Testament names are very often used Romany Gypsies – though also by Puritans. It is not an exact science.

22

British Isles Surnames in Australia and New Zealand

In 1770 James Cook claimed Australia for Britain, and migration from the British Isles started soon afterwards. New Zealand, visited by James Cook on the same voyage, was not formally incorporated within the British Empire until 1840, though settlement had begun a little before.

AUSTRALIA

The 20 most common surnames of Australia (2007) are (in order): Smith, Jones, Williams, Brown, Wilson, Taylor, Johnson, White, Martin, Anderson, Thompson, Nguyen, Thomas, Walker, Harris, Lee, Ryan, Robinson, Kelly and King. With the exception of Nguyen – a Vietnamese surname which is borne by around 40% of Vietnamese – these names may all be from the British Isles and therefore reflect the British Isles ancestry of most people now living in Australia. Lee comprises both the British Isles surname and the common Chinese surname Li/Lee. Johnson and Anderson are both British and Swedish in origin.

In Australia roughly one person in 200 has the surname Smith, a higher frequency than in the British Isles. This suggests that the migrants with the surname of Smith have been joined by migrants with other surnames changing their name, seeking the incognito of Smith alongside their new life in Australia. Irish names are common in Australia, for example Ryan and Kelly, reflecting the high levels of migration from Ireland to Australia, particularly at the time of the Potato Famine (1845–1852).

Johnson (7) and Anderson (10), both score more highly than at first might be expected. In the British Isles these patronymics are common – Johnson particularly in the north of England, and Anderson particularly in Scotland. However, this is not a sufficient explanation for their high ranking in Australia. The solution is that as well as being British Isles surnames these names are spelling variants of Johansson and Andersson, the two most common surnames in Sweden. Around one Swede in 20 today has one of these two names. In Australia the surname primarily reflects the migrations from Sweden to Australia.

Transportation to Australia

Australia started as a penal colony, with many of the first settlers taken from the gaols of the British Isles for a sentence of convict labour in Australia. Transportation to Australia often disrupted surnames, or even created an environment in which new surnames might arise. At the simplest migrants might have wished to make a new start. However, more complex surname formation environments existed. Take for example the case of Amy Staples, born 1775 in Sutton-at-Hone, Kent, who entered domestic service in London. In 1801 she was convicted (on circumstantial evidence) for petty theft from her employer, and sentenced to death, subsequently commuted because she was pregnant to transportation to Australia. In the course of a harsh life in Australia it is possible to imagine that Sutton came to be remembered as some lost Eden, and as a result one of her grandchildren was given the name Sutton as an additional surname. Sutton certainly exists as an English surname, but this represents a new coinage in Australia.

New Zealand

British settlement of New Zealand is mostly subsequent to 1840, with much of the migration taking place in the late 19th century and throughout the 20th century. There was a significant degree of integration with the indigenous Maori population, leading to coinage of surnames in the British Isles system by families of Maori origin.

All parts of the British Isles are represented in the settlement of New Zealand, though some more than others. In general there are more English and fewer Welsh, Scottish and Irish names in New Zealand than in most parts of the world where British people settled, a circumstance which reflects the relatively late date of settlement of New Zealand. Non-English surnames tend to be localized: Scottish surnames show a focus on Clydeside and Irish surnames on Ulster, suggesting migration from the ports of Glasgow and Belfast. Unsurprisingly the most common surname today in New Zealand is Smith.

Earlier settlers to New Zealand came not only from the British Isles but also from elsewhere in Europe (including significant groups from Dalmatia and Bohemia) as well as from the USA and India, while from the 1870s and 1880s there was migration from China's Guangdong province.

The Maori people of New Zealand traditionally did not use surnames. Under British influence they at first adopted not surnames but patronymics, with the patronymic changing for each generation. However, from the early 20th century surnames in the British tradition were established. The extensive inter-marriage between Maori and British people has led to a situation where many have simply adopted a British-origin surname. Alternatively what was once a Maori first name may be used as a surname, and sometimes with both a Maori form and an anglicized form being used together, so that a person may have alternate surnames and choose to stress either their Maori or British heritage by the version they use.

ACTIVITY

Australian surnames

▶ Australian surnames and Australian genealogy are closely linked. The goal for most investigating surnames and families in Australia is to identify the founder of the Australian family. In view of the relatively recent date of settlement and the high quality and good availability of Australian vital records, this is usually possible. Any of the many books and magazines on Australian genealogy or the many websites available will show how this can be done.

▶ The story of the penal settlements in Australia is covered by books such as Michael Flynn's *The Second Fleet: Britain's Grim Convict Armada of 1790*. This contains the biographies of 1,500 convicts, seamen and soldiers who travelled to New South Wales. In effect it gives a list of many of the first surnames to be brought to Australia.

ACTIVITY

New Zealand surnames

▶ Resources are available for tracing New Zealand genealogy, and it is usually possible to identify an ancestor who was the first to settle in New Zealand. The migration is on average later than in Australia, and in very many cases such information is remembered by families.

▶ Work specifically on New Zealand surnames is surprisingly scant. Distribution patterns within New Zealand are not generally available – though using techniques described in this book you can make your own. Even work on frequency seems disappointing – though again you can make your own study. The area of Maori adoption of surnames offers much that it is intriguing, and surprisingly little that has been done. For an enthusiast somewhere this is a rich area for study.

23

British Isles Surnames in the Americas

British settlement of the Americas dates from the *Mayflower* voyage of the Pilgrim Fathers in 1620, and the very first British surnames in the Americas are those of the *Mayflower* pilgrims and their fellow travellers. Migration gathered pace in the following centuries. While most British surnames in North America indeed indicate British Isles ancestry, these roots are often far more recent than the era of the Pilgrim Fathers.

CANADA

The ten most common surnames in Canada are Li, Smith, Lam, Martin, Brown, Roy, Tremblay, Lee, Gagnon and Wilson. Several of these are not of British Isles origin. Li is from China (and Lee frequently a spelling variant), while Lam is a Cantonese surname particularly associated with Hong Kong. Tremblay is the most common surname in Quebec, and of French origin. Gagnon is similarly of French origin, a distinctive Quebec version of French Gagné. One family in Quebec joins the two as Gagnon-Tremblay, surely the most Quebecoise name that could be imagined.

Almost all of the European settlement of Canada took place in the last three centuries, sufficiently recent for the original settlement patterns to have an impact on present-day surname distributions. For example, Yorkshire surnames in Canada are particularly common in Nova Scotia. This is a result of a specific migration in 1772–1775 by which Nova Scotia received an influx of around 1,000 people from Yorkshire, bringing with them Yorkshire surnames.

All parts of the British Isles are represented in Canadian British Isles surnames. The circumstance where England has the highest population of any of the nations of the British Isles is reflected in a preponderance of English surnames.

UNITED STATES OF AMERICA

The surnames of British Isles origins represented in the USA are an uneven reflection of those in the British Isles. The surname homes most often encountered are those from areas from which migrants came, which means that Ireland is especially well represented. By contrast, the surnames of northern England are rather unusual in the USA – so surnames of British origin ending in *–son* are nowhere near as frequent as in the British Isles. Thus for example Wilkinson is a common surname in the British Isles with its origin in the north of England, and is ranked at 72 in England and Wales, yet in the USA it is well down the list, ranked at 631.

The USA takes surnames from many sources as well as from the British Isles. Often these have been modified to resemble the British system. This may be just a spelling change – a Scandinavian Jonsson to Johnson – or the change may be more ambitious as migrants to the USA sought to fit in and be inconspicuous. Often English spellings of names were adopted, so for example Van Rosevelt became Roosevelt, and Roggenfelder became Rockefeller. Such forms are essentially names created within the USA. Also common is the translation of surnames.

Smith is of course common in the USA, as in all English-speaking countries. While in the USA the surname Smith may be from a British Isles ancestor by this name, it may also be a translation of a surname meaning 'smith' from many European languages. These include Schmid(t) (German), Lefevre (French), McGowan (Gaelic), Kovacs (Hungarian), Kuznetsov (Russian), Kowalsky (Ukrainian), Kowalski (Polish), Kalvaitis (Lithuanian), Seppanen (Finnish), and doubtless many more.

FORMER SLAVES

Very many African Americans whose ancestors were slaves bear surnames of British Isles origin. Various legal codes denied slaves a surname on the grounds that they were perceived as having no legal father and being the property of the slave owner. Typically the christening records of babies who were born into slavery show only a first name. On obtaining their freedom, former slaves needed a surname, and usually adopted a surname from within the British Isles name stock.

Popular accounts suggest that freed slaves took the surnames of their former owners. While there are doubtless occasions when this happened, manumission registers from the West Indies suggest that this practice was not at all common, and there is little in the way of support for the idea that this was the usual practice anywhere. In most cases it is probably right to look elsewhere for surname origins.

■ As slaves had no surnames it was common to give two first names so that the individual could be identified, as John James or John Moses. Following manumission it was often convenient for the second forename to be used as if a surname, giving surnames such as James and Moses. Sometimes what was perceived as a surname form of a first name was used, so Williams, Jackson. A woman former slave may similarly adopt a female first name as a surname, and give this surname to her children, so Mary or Jane. This appears to be the main source of unaltered female first names used as surnames.

- Many former slaves appear to have chosen from the most common surnames around them, effectively seeking an incognito. Smith, Jones, Brown and Davis are typical.

- Many former slaves took the name of someone they respected, often an abolitionist. Many members of the Quaker 'underground railway' that helped slaves escape the southern states of the USA are so honoured. Hopkins, Mullins, Wilson and Wright appear to be from this source, at least on occasions.

- Occasionally, freed slaves adopted the name of the place where a legal process of manumission was carried out.

Most freed slaves exercised choice in the surname they adopted. There is the story of William, a man born a slave in Kentucky in 1817, who ran away, heading for Canada. Caught in the winter snows without food, shoes or adequate clothing and close to death, he was helped by a Quaker, Wells Brown, who provided a fortnight's shelter, as well as shoes, clothes and money to continue his journey. William later chose as his surname Wells Brown.

ACTIVITY

The genealogical record
Genealogical records for the USA and Canada are of a high standard and accessible. For very many families it is possible to trace a line back to the migrant ancestor. Very many such migrant ancestors are as

recent as the early 20th or late 19th centuries, so the task is of manageable proportions. If you want to know about a point of surname origin in North America, trace it!

For USA genealogy start with the *Family History and Genealogy* section at **www.usa.gov/**. For Canadian genealogy start with *Canadian Genealogy*, **www.canadian-genealogy.org/**

ACTIVITY

Ellis Island
Very many of the migrants to the USA – certainly a representative cross-section – entered through the Port of New York, through Ellis Island. Records are now available for free online at *Ellis Island, The Port of New York*, **www.ellisisland.org**, comprising around 25 million travellers. Useful searches include:

▶ for a specific name if you are looking for a known ancestor;

▶ by surname alone to gain an idea of the frequency of that name – the records display at 25 per screen, and if your search result fits on just one screen it is a most unusual migrant surname;

▶ by a group of surnames from one US locality to see whether the settlers came at around the same time and from the same location.

ACTIVITY

Slave ancestors
For many Americans today the generation of slavery was that of their great-grandparents or great-great-grandparents, still well within the time-frame of family tradition. It is reasonable to expect to be able to find the ancestor who first adopted a particular surname, and perhaps work out why. A starting point is *My Slave Ancestors*, **www.myslaveancestors.com/**

24

Dealing with Extinct Surnames

Most surnames, once started, grew exponentially as the population increased. Yet there is an intriguing catalogue of surnames that got started, flourished and then, amazingly, died out entirely.

THE BLACK DEATH

The single greatest cause of surname extinction in the British Isles is the Black Death of 1348–1350. Occurring just at a time when many surnames were becoming established, this was a tragedy that could wipe out all male members of a family and therefore whole surnames.

This epidemic we call the Black Death was a worldwide bubonic plague, starting in China around 1340. In England the population plunged from around 4 million or more to somewhere just over 2 million, therefore with somewhere close to one person in two dying. Exact figures aren't available. Some areas were more badly hit than others, with some villages completely destroyed by the plague. East Anglia as a whole was very badly hit, and Aston (Birmingham) lost around 80% of its population. Around a thousand English villages entirely ceased to exist. Any survivors of these villages fled them to make their lives elsewhere. For Scotland, Wales and Ireland figures are less certain, but the death toll was broadly comparable – about half the population died.

A consequence of the Black Death was that many families perished in their entirety. At an age when surnames were just coming into existence and where a particular surname may have had the few people bearing it all living in one locality, it was possible to have a surname lost.

As well as actual family extinction and surname extinction the Black Death created a climate of fear – fear of death of self, of family, of village. The plague returned every decade or so from the first outbreak, with a further 10–15% of the population dying in the 1361–2 pandemic. An aspect of the fear was that people sought a form of immortality through their children. The practice of fathers having a son who bore precisely their name (and to a lesser extent mothers and daughters) is largely a development of this period. Where a man did not have a son the custom developed of leaving an estate to an heir descended through the female line, often a son-in-law, nephew or grandson, on the condition that they were prepared to trade their name with that of the deceased. Surnames may on occasions therefore travel in unexpected ways in order to avoid extinction of a name. This late-14th and early 15th-century practice resurfaced in the 17th and 18th centuries and has been found occasionally in other centuries.

SHAMEFUL NAMES

Some names have died of shame – literally! Examples are the now extinct surnames Morville, Muschet and Plonker.

Notorious names

Morville has a clear origin in Hugh de Morville, an Anglo-Norman knight who died in 1162, and whose name relates to an estate in Normandy. He gained Scottish estates in Cunningham and

Lauderdale, and served as Constable of Scotland, which meant he was in charge of the king's bodyguard. His son Richard stepped into his illustrious shoes, and the surname seemed well established. Another son, Hugh, was Lord of Westmorland. In 1170 with three other knights, this second Hugh de Morville assassinated the Archbishop of Canterbury Thomas Becket in Canterbury Cathedral. The action launched Becket on the path to sainthood, with his tomb in Canterbury Cathedral the most popular medieval English pilgrimage site. The murderers became the subject of popular vilification, and their surnames came to be avoided. Those represented by the other knights – Reginald Fitzurse, William de Tracy and Richard le Breton – have not prospered and are today rare, though Fitzurse, Tracy and Breton do exist. Morville by contrast seems to have died out completely in the British Isles. Curiously it exists in America, though presumably of a different origin, possibly Danish.

Figure 24. The murderers of Thomas Becket shown here on the Palencia Reliquary were reviled by their age and the surname of one died from the shame.

Muschet was the surname of a family established in Perthshire and Stirlingshire, and found from at least the 14th century through to the early 18th century, by which time there must have been many hundreds of bearers of the surname. And then it vanished in the British Isles. Almost overnight every one of the hundreds of bearers of this long-established name decided to change it. The reason is that one of the last generation of bearers of the name was Nicol Muschet of Boghall who was executed by hanging in Edinburgh in 1721 'for the horrid and bloody murder of his own wife'. The case was notorious. Margaret, his wife, was just 17 years old when her throat was cut by a drunken Nicol Muschet. Prior to his execution he made a public confession of his sin, while subsequently his friends published an elegy setting out both his 'lewd life' and 'pious end' – these circumstances leading to yet more interest in the case. Even a century later Nicol Muschet was remembered, and may be a source for the anti-hero in James Hogg's novel *The Private Memoirs and Confessions of a Justified Sinner*. Nicol Muschet was a name on everyone's tongue. Seemingly the taint of the name Muschet was so great that all of the many hundreds of people who bore it felt obliged to change their name, a circumstance which today is hard to comprehend. Presumably numerous genealogical searches are blocked around 1721 because of the Muschet name change.

Offensive names

Plonker was well established in the 16th and 17th centuries, particularly in Surrey. It is from the place name Ploquenet in Brittany. Yet in the early 1700s it died out completely. The reason is surely that the word 'plonker' had evolved with an unsavoury slang meaning. The earliest recorded use of the slang word 'plonker' dates from the First World War, when it was highly offensive (it has subsequently moderated in meaning so it does not cause the offence today it once did). However, the demise of the surname Plonker suggests that the slang word existed at least 200 years earlier than its first known usage. Many called Plonker simply modified their name to the innocuous Plunkett. Similarly the Shetland surname Twatt has in most cases been replaced by the innocuous Watt.

ILLEGAL NAMES

On occasions names have been made illegal. This is particularly a feature of Scots law where it is termed *proscription*. The process should lead to surname extinction, yet it appears notable for its ineffectiveness.

Surely the most infamous case is that of the Clan MacDonald of Glencoe. As a result of the sloth of their clan chief in swearing an oath of allegiance, the decision was made to make an example of them, and the order given was:

> You are hereby ordered to fall upon the rebels, the McDonalds of Glenco, and put all to the sword under seventy. You are to have a special care that the old Fox and his sons doe upon no account escape your hands, you are to secure all the avenues that no man escape.

The massacre of 1692 through which this order was implemented killed 78 of the Clan MacDonald, and few today can claim descent from a MacDonald of Glencoe. The surname MacDonald has survived because there were MacDonalds not living in Glencoe.

One of the most remarkable surname stories in the British Isles is that of MacGregor, which was proscribed from 1603 until 1775, meaning that it was actually illegal to use this surname. The proscription was a punishment for a clan that was considered to be outside the law:

> the bare and simple name of McGregor made that whole clan to presume of their power, force and strength, and did encourage them...to go forth in their iniquities.
>
> James VI King of Scots, *Act of Council*, 1603

ROB ROY.

FROM AN ORIGINAL DRAWING

Figure 25. Among the many crimes of Highland outlaw Rob Roy Mac-Gregor was that he dared to use his surname, a name then illegal in Scots law.

So severe were the penalties that the wonder is that there is anyone today who bears this name. Certainly for this 172 years no one could openly use the name MacGregor. Most famous of the MacGregors during the years of proscription is Rob Roy MacGregor, otherwise Rob Roy Campbell, the outlaw made famous by dozens of stories and by the novel of Walter Scott. All Mac-Gregors changed their name, at least for official purposes, and many adopted the names Campbell, Graham, Stewart, and Drummond, all clans with whom the MacGregors were linked. We have on record that in 1695 Evan MacGregor petitioned the Scottish parliament against the proscription of his surname and was granted special permission to use MacGregor for his own lifetime, but was required to give his children a different surname. He chose for them a patronymic based on his first name, with his children called Evanson.

Yet today despite proscription the surname MacGregor is well established in the British Isles. It is hard to escape the view that previous generations for the most part knew far more about their ancestry than many do today, and that reversion to the traditional form of ancestors five or six generations previous was a matter of pride. The MacGregors claim descent from a Gregor who lived in the 14th century, a true father of his clan. In fact DNA evidence doesn't quite support this. There certainly is a single common ancestor for the MacGregors, but he lived at least a century earlier than Gregor. What we seem to have is an early clan structure of related families all with patrilinear descent from a common ancestor who in the 14th century were led by a Gregor, and who adopted the name MacGregor in order to emphasize their kinship. MacGregors are related but not in quite the way they think.

Misspelt names

Very many cases of apparently extinct names are simply spelling variants or spelling mistakes. Thus for example the 1861 census appears to show the existence of the surname Persgovet, a name which subsequently vanishes, yet closer analysis shows this is in fact a wrong spelling for Peasgood. It only ever existed in the mind of the census official. Victorian records are certainly full of errors, including wrong spellings of surnames, and census returns are particularly prone to such mistakes as the document was completed not by the informant but by the enumerator, who often wrote down what he thought he heard. Enumerators were poorly paid, and often less than scrupulous in their work. A strange name on just one census return probably reflects just a mistake. However, a strange spelling on multiple census returns and in the registers of birth, marriage and death does indicate a genuine name. There is always the possibility that the genuine name has arisen as a result of a misspelling becoming formalized.

One such is the surname Moulting, which is well documented in the 19th century, yet found neither before nor since. The origin of this surname is explicable – it appears to be a variant of Moulton – but the circumstance where it completely vanishes is hard to explain. In view of the large size of 19th-century families it seems beyond belief that the male line should have failed in its entirety. There is of course a certain humour in Moulting, though such a circumstance has not prevented the survival of other comical surnames. Possibly some bearers were aware of the origin of the name and deliberately reverted it. Notwithstanding, it is surprising that there is not a single Moulting in the British Isles today – unless of course you know differently.

ACTIVITY

Watch your spelling

You are most likely to encounter an apparently extinct surname in a Victorian census return or in an 18th-century parish register. The first stage in examining it must be to see whether it is a genuine extinct name. Try the following.

▷ It is usually straightforward to follow a family through the ten-yearly census returns. An 'extinct' surname in just one census suggests that the census enumerator simply spelt what he thought he heard and got it wrong. By contrast, the same spelling in two or more census years (or in districts of the same census enumerated by a different man) may suggest a genuine, extinct surname. Note that the 1911 census return was (mostly) completed by the individual householders, who should have had a good idea how their name was spelt.

▷ Look at 19th-century vital records (birth, marriage and death). Much more care was taken in compiling these records and there are far fewer mistakes. In particular, marriage records tend to have accurate spellings – as well as the bride and groom there were two witnesses, and frequently family and friends of both, and very often someone knew how a name should be spelt.

▶ Eighteenth-century parish registers were compiled by vicars who were often newcomers to the parish. They didn't know how a surname should be spelt, guessed the first time it was necessary to record it, and copied their guess subsequently. Check that an 'extinct' surname is recorded by more than one person.

ACTIVITY

Explaining the extinction of a name
Names don't just die out. There has to be a reason. Look for evidence of the following:

▶ The Black Death

▶ A localized calamity that wiped out a recent-origin surname. For example, a shipwreck has the potential to kill all male members of a surname first recorded in the British Isles only a generation or two beforehand.

▶ Excommunication of a bearer of the name creating a taint which encouraged everyone to change their name.

▶ A notorious murderer is a bearer of the name.

▶ The name was made illegal.

▶ The name was German and changed around the time of the two world wars.

25

Investigating DNA Studies

One part of the human genome, the Y-chromosome, is passed from father to son. The transmission direction is not identical to that of surnames (which pass from father to both sons and daughters) but mirrors the key patrilinear descent. The basic concept is that people related through the same male-line ancestry should have identical Y-chromosomes. Men with the same monogenetic surname should be related.

DNA studies also give a way into the much broader area of the study of ethnicity. Here Y-chromosome studies are complemented by studies of mitochondrial DNA (which passes from mother to children, boys as well as girls).

THE GENES OF THE BRITISH ISLES

The genetics of the population of the British Isles is dominated by two groups. First are the genes of the peoples who entered the British Isles as the last Ice Age ended. These are well represented and are the dominant genetic legacy of the British Isles. This genetic type is usually called Celtic, though the name is at best misleading and arguably simply wrong. Rather it is a pre-Celtic genetic legacy. By contrast, the Celtic migrants who brought their language and culture to the British Isles left an almost undetectable genetic legacy, with the result that Central European Celtic genes are very rare in the British Isles.

Then alongside the pre-Celtic or 'Celtic' genes are the Germanic genes of the Anglo-Saxon, Viking and Norman invaders of the early Middle Ages. These are effectively one genetic type – certainly Anglo-Saxon and Danish Viking cannot be distinguished, and Danish Viking is the dominant genetic heritage both of the Viking age and of the Norman Conquest (reflecting the original Danish homeland of the Normans). Some have felt that they can distinguish Norwegian Viking genes from other Germanic genes and certainly there is now quite a literature around this topic; my own view is that they are chasing a will of the wisp.

Of course there are many other genes in the British Isles mix. But in simple terms there are two clear genetic types, the pre-Celtic ('Celtic') and the Germanic. There are also areas of the British Isles where one type or other greatly predominates and has done for more than a thousand years. Thus for example the West Coast of Ireland is where pre-Celtic ('Celtic') predominates while East Anglia is where Germanic predominates. These two types once displayed different characteristics – for example, two types of facial characteristics. Pre-Celtic ('Celtic') tended to be wide, round faces with a relatively large chin (the brachycephalic skull type) while Germanic tend to be narrow, long faces with prominent cheekbones and a small chin (the dolichocephalic type).

There is some degree of mapping of genetic types on to surnames. This cannot be through Y-chromosome inheritance alone; rather it is because a family originates from one area where one type or the other is most common. To a limited extent it works, yet there are very many exceptions.

THE GENES OF REAL ANCESTORS

The Y-chromosome is usually passed from father to son without change, so all men related through the male line should have an identical Y-chromosome. However, once in a while a mutation occurs which differentiates a Y-chromosome from all others. It becomes possible to postulate the existence of an individual who was the first to have a particular Y-chromosome. Frequently these are within the period when surnames have existed, so we are making real progress in mapping surnames on to Y-chromosome patterns.

Just what can and cannot be achieved is indicated by a variety of examples.

- The technique offers a way of exploring a legend. It is asserted that all Koreans are descended from a single man, someone who really would be a true father of a nation. This assertion is readily tested by sampling the Y-chromosomes of ethnic Koreans. There is a clear result – it has been disproved. There is no single male founder of the Korean people.

- Similarly it is asserted by the Jewish faith that all members of the Jewish hereditary priesthood – the *cohanim* – are descendants of one man, Aaron the brother of Moses. Descent is patrilinear and may never pass through a woman. Today the surnames Cohen, Kahn, Kane are borne by people who are themselves hereditary priests (cohen), or who claim descent from an ancestor who was a cohen. It is therefore possible to speculate that if the story is correct men who bear Cohen or a related surname should share a distinctive Y-chromosome. Amazingly, Y-chromosome analysis has confirmed this origin – or at least genetic testing has been consistent with the story,

Figure 26. DNA has demonstrated that it is probable that many with the surname Cohen are descendants of Aaron, brother of Moses – shown in this image from Vatopedi Monastery, Mount Athos.

showing that just over half of men who are called Cohen (etc.) are in fact descended from one man at about a 3,000–4,000 year removal from the present, a date which corresponds with the time of Aaron. Additionally it has shown that a further 15% have a comparable Y-chromosome which may reflect a later chromosomal mutation by one individual. In broad-brush terms around two-thirds of people bearing a form of the surname Cohen are related, and have a common ancestor whom we may plausibly call Aaron. Their surname therefore reflects the longest genetically proved pedigree from a named individual.

■ The Clan Donald claims descent from the Norse King Somerled (died 1164). The idea is that everyone in the Clan Donald, whether their surname is MacDonald, MacAlistair, MacDougall or one of the less common surnames of the clan, shares a common ancestor. Can this be right? Well maybe. A DNA study based on the surname MacDonald – now borne by around two million people globally – has concluded that about

400,000 are descended from a common ancestor and therefore carry Somerled's Y-chromosome. There is a long tradition by which successful Scottish clans such as the Clan Donald have given their surnames to retainers and supporters (who frequently intermarried with the clan), while descent of the surname through the female line has been relatively common. Both these features reduce the chances of a patrilinear common ancestor. Indeed it is probably surprising that at a remove of around 30 generations as many as 20% of present MacDonalds show the Somerled Y-chromosome. Additionally, very many bearers of the MacDonald name who are without this particular Y-chromosome are nonetheless related, though through the female line. If your surname is MacDonald there is a fair chance that Somerled really is your ancestor.

GENES AND SURNAMES

The basic idea is that one surname may have one genetic profile. It works. Numerous British Isles studies have produced outstanding results. One of the most striking is around the surname Sykes. Sykes appears to be a place name in origin. The word is a Yorkshire term for a drainage ditch and is an element in several place names, including Sykehouse. A study by Bryan Sykes and Catherine Irven[2] has demonstrated a single origin for Sykes. All who bear this name are likely to be related through the male line. This relatively common surname has therefore been shown to be monogenetic. It gives credence to the view that very many surnames, even relatively common ones, are monogenetic, and may suggest that even many of our most common surnames arose

---

2 'Surnames and the Y Chromosome', *Journal of the American Society of Human Genetics*, vol. 66, 2000.

quite a small number of times. Sykes today is the name of around 25,000 people in the UK (extrapolated from electoral registers) all of whom can reasonably assume they are related – truly a big family.

Work in pairing surnames with Y-chromosomes has been carried out by Mark Jobling and Turi King in the Department of Genetics at Leicester University. They have demonstrated that there is an observable correlation between surnames and relationship. In broad-brush terms two people born in the British Isles with the same surname have about a one in four chance of being related through patrilinear descent. The odds are much longer with the most common surnames, particularly Smith and Jones, but conversely for uncommon surnames the chance rises to about one in two. Where there is a common location for the known ancestors the chances rise still further. Two broad conclusions can be drawn:

- the vast majority of surnames are monogenetic – they arose just once;

- in British Isles society for the last thousand years the overwhelming majority of children are the children of the acknowledged father.

Both these conclusions are stunning. The monogenetic nature of most of our surnames has not generally been recognized. The propriety of family relationships has not previously been demonstrated in quite this way. Additionally the outstanding result for the Cohen demonstrates three millennia – perhaps a hundred generations – where the acknowledged father is the genetic father.

WHEN GENES FAIL TO SHOW RELATIONSHIP

One circumstance where the surname did not (usually) pass from father to child is when the child was born out of wedlock. In such circumstances most children adopted their mother's surname. While sons do not carry the Y-chromosome of their maternal grandfather, they do have as much genetic heritage from this ancestry as from any others. Therefore even when the Y-chromosome is not that associated with the surname it is still possible that other genetic heritage is, and that people are related.

Statistics for the chance of relationship with others bearing the surname are not yet available. However, the following rule of thumb may be explored. For surnames which are not common (say not in the top 100) it is probable that almost all who bore that name born before 1800 were related. The proviso of 'born before 1800' leaves out the disruptions caused by the mobile populations of the last two centuries.

ACTIVITY

Considering a DNA test
DNA tests are now very easy to source and modest in price. Most are postal services using a self-administered cheek swab for the DNA sample.

▶ Many companies offer genealogical DNA testing. You need to find the right one for you. For a Y-chromosome test you need a company that has many users in the part of the world that your paternal ancestors come from.

▶ Only men have a Y-chromosome. Women may wish to consider asking a male relative – a brother, father or paternal uncle for example – to take the test. However, the results will be delivered to this individual, not a different person who pays for the test.

▶ Companies take steps to preserve your privacy. Notwithstanding, if you have a DNA test your information is 'out there' and there is a theoretical possibility of it being abused.

▶ Be aware that if two members of a family take a genealogical DNA test it is possible that it will show that the two are not related as they think they are. For example, two male cousins related through the male line should have the same Y-chromosome – if they don't there is something wrong with the family tree they believe exists. There are plenty of possibilities of upsets.

▶ For best results it is likely to be necessary to have a more extensive DNA test than the minimum offered by any test supplier.

▶ DNA tests have the potential to give information on ethnicity. However, most don't as a default option – if this is the information you particularly want you need to source a test which offers it.

ACTIVITY

Are you a caveman or a cavewoman?
A stunning case of Y-chromosome transmission is the case of Adrian Targett of the village of Cheddar (Somerset). He knew his paternal ancestry to be from the area and the surname Targett localises well with Somerset. It would be reasonable to assume that his Y-chromosome was from Somerset, perhaps even from the Celtic people who pre-date the Anglo-Saxon shire of Somerset. Yet everyone was stunned when geneticist Bill Sykes managed to link his Y-chromosome with DNA extracted from the remains of prehistoric 'Cheddar Man', a caveman and hunter living in the area around 9,000 years ago. Adrian Targett is in the special position of knowing he is a direct male-line descendant of a caveman whose Y-chromosome he carries. Amazingly he lives just 300 yards from the cave in which Cheddar Man was discovered, so given around 300 generations separating the two men, his family has moved an average of 36 inches a generation.

Unless you are part of a very special study you will have no chance of replicating such a finding. But a mitochondrial DNA study should be able to identify a distant female ancestor. The human family tree has passed through a genetic bottleneck consisting of a very small number of women (and presumably a similar number of men) who are ancestors of all of us. For the women – called the 'daughters of Eve' – we know something about where they lived and when. It is possible for all of us to find out about this key individual on our maternal line of descent. We can all have a personal link with prehistory.

One-Name Studies

Very many surnames have produced a society dedicated to investigating the family of the surname. Often they are the less common surnames.

Guild of One-Name Studies

The pre-eminent organization for the study of single surnames is the Guild of One-Name Studies. Its foundation in 1979 was low key, with the organization's acronym – GOONS – deliberately chosen as a self-deprecating name reflecting the eccentric interests of the members. It has been successful beyond expectations, and has remodelled itself as a more serious organization – indeed it no longer uses the acronym GOONS. It is a charity receiving income both from members and from the Halsted Trust, an educational charity with the brief 'to advance the education of the public in the study of and research into family history, genealogy, heraldry and local history through one-name studies generally, but in particular with reference to all persons having the surname of Halsted, and to promote the preservation, security and publication of the useful results of such research.' Halsted is now the most studied single surname ever.

Curiously the extensive work on Halsted has so far not managed to identify a single progenitor. Rather it has identified discrete branches of the family originating in Lancashire, Cumberland, Yorkshire, Essex and Sussex. The earliest form of the surname appears to be de Hallstedes in the early 14th century. The work demonstrates both what can be done – and the material on Halsted is impressively extensive – and also the limitations of what can be done. It now seems most unlikely that a single Halsted progenitor will be identified, not because such a person didn't exist but because the necessary records have not survived.

The Register of One-Name Studies

The Guild of One-Name Studies maintains the Register of One-Name Studies. This is exactly what its name suggests – a list of groups researching a single surname. For those surnames registered by the Guild the information amassed is often extensive, and significant contributions are being made to the study of surnames.

Creating spurious links

The work of the Guild of One-Name Studies has been criticized in that it treats together what may be several different families, and may therefore imply a spurious link simply because they bear the same surname. Yet such criticism hardly seems justified. In order to determine whether families really are distinct or part of the same family it is precisely the sort of work the Guild is involved in which needs to be undertaken.

Going global

The intention of the Guild of One-Name Studies is to research all occurrences of a particular surname anywhere in the world. The remit is in theory global, but so far there is a clear focus on the British Isles and on those countries to which British people migrated. This is a much broader remit than purely family tree research (though there is a significant overlap).

■ The Guild often gets as close as it is possible to get to the origin of surnames.

■ Very many surnames are being shown to be predominantly monogenetic, or to have a defined small number of points of origin.

A one-name study may be a way around a genealogical block. Investigating all occurrences of a particular name provides a context for the block, perhaps suggesting a place of origin for the individual concerned. One-name studies are undoubtedly a valuable genealogical tool.

ACTIVITY

Exploring one-name studies

▶ Is the surname you are interested in covered by the Guild of One-Name Studies? Their web site is **www.one-name.org**. If so, you've hit the jackpot – crack open the champagne!

▶ If it isn't, consider offering a surname study. After reading this book you are well on the way to being an expert. This is a way of sharing your work with the world and making contact with others with similar interests.

Taking Charge of Your Surname

Within the British Isles it has long been customary for women to adopt their husband's surname on marriage. Changes of surname in other circumstances are still relatively unusual. Yet there is no reason why this should be the case.

DOUBLE-BARRELLED NAMES

A simple way to change a surname is to put two together. Double-barrelled surnames are rare before the Victorian age. During the Victorian age and for the 20th century most were formed when the mother's maiden name was added before the father's surname. If John Jones married Mary Smith the children might be called Smith Jones. The surname was indexed under Jones, with Smith effectively relegated to the status of a middle name. Occasionally the name was hyphenated, as Smith-Jones, which in effect prioritized the mother's surname, as this is how it would be indexed. Hyphens were rare before around 1870 and have now largely gone out of fashion for the formation of new names, so the hyphen represents a surname formation within little more than a century, roughly 1870 to 1990. Sometimes the additional surname came from a godparent or similar, and need not be a family surname. The Victorian age also developed the tradition of an illegitimate child being given the father's surname before the mother's, with or without the father's consent. In such cases the surname was usually not hyphenated, so the child's name was indexed under the mother's name.

It is possible in theory to combine a double-barrelled name with a third surname, producing a triple-barrelled name, though very rare. It is even possible to combine two or more double- or triple-barrelled names. The longest English surname which I know is Plantagenet-Temple-Nugent-Brydges-Chandos-Greville, the surname of Richard, the 1st Duke of Buckingham.

Today it is increasingly common for children to be given their mother's surname as their final name, with the father's name as a middle name – and the name is not hyphenated. The intention is sometimes that children as they become adults may choose one or other surname.

Attitudes to double-barrelled surnames have changed markedly. A generation ago the practice was considered to be largely a custom of the upper-middle and upper class. Now it is frequent across society.

DO YOU LIKE YOUR SURNAME?

Few of us have chosen the surname we bear. Yet many surnames are carried with pride because of the positive associations they have. Frequently these are some of the very oldest surnames. From England these might be names such as Percy, Spencer and Montgomery, all long-established and all with aristocratic associations. Similarly Scotland has such names as Gordon, Sinclair, Douglas, Campbell, and Macleod, again long-established and the names of leading figures in the history of Scotland, and also the names of large clans. From Ireland such surnames as O'Brien and O'Neil are a source of pride for their origins in early medieval Ireland. Though it was acquired merely by chance, very many people like their surname.

For each of us our name is an integral part of our identity. Yet some people do change their names – and sometimes with good reason.

CHANGING A SURNAME

Within the British Isles changing a surname is straightforward. Most changes are made using a deed poll plus an advertisement, which is the simplest method. Alternatively it is possible to dispense with this legal process and simply inform all appropriate authorities of the change. For those investigating surname changes in the British Isles in the last 300 years or so there is no single source of information – indeed many changes will have been effected simply by a change in usage. For those formally changed many have an advertisement in *The Times* (which is now available online). Others – particularly those 18th- and 19th-century changes that went through a process of change by Royal License – may be recorded in the *London Gazette* or *Dublin Gazette* (both covering the whole of the British Isles). Many 18th- and 19th-century changes were made on succeeding to property where adopting the benefactor's surname was a condition of inheriting.

Changing a name simply because it is too common is probably not necessary in the British Isles. Even our most common surnames are not so common as to cause real problems in identification. By contrast, in Denmark in 1903 a law was passed encouraging name change, motivated by a circumstance where surnames such as Hansen, Petersen and Sorensen were extremely common – for example one person in ten in Copenhagen was then called Hansen.

The name changes with which we are most familiar are those made by media celebrities. Thus Derek Gentron Gaspart Ulric van den Bogaerde changed his name to Dirk Bogarde, Greta Gustafsson to Greta Garbo and Frances Gumm to Judy Garland. Authors have traditionally shown a propensity to change their name, such as Charles Lutwidge Dodgson to Lewis Carol (here the etymology is good – Lutwidge and Lewis are cognate, as are Charles and Carol). Joanne Rowling, Harry Potter author, was persuaded by her publisher to use initials rather than first name so as not to alienate boy readers, and as she doesn't have a middle name she adopted a middle initial, becoming J. K. Rowling.

PSYCHOLOGY AND SURNAMES

There is a wider issue around the psychological effect of surnames upon both their bearers and others. One of the few studies of the topic is by Christopher Bagley and Louise Evan-Wong,[3] which demonstrates that children do evaluate their own names and those of others and respond to those judgements.

Undesirable surnames

Some names for a variety of reasons are simply undesirable. An extreme case is the surname Raper. This is an occupational name with the meaning of rope-maker, cognate with Roper. The

3 'Psychiatric Disorder and Adult and Peer Group Rejection of the Child's Name', *Journal of Child Psychology and Psychiatry*, 11.1, 2006.

spelling Raper is strongly associated with Yorkshire and reflects a regional pronunciation. The development of the common noun 'raper' (as a form of *rapist* and replacing the older *ravisher*) has made the surname undesirable. If an individual is comfortable with the surname for themselves then it seems to me that it is reasonable to applaud their ability to rise above an unfortunate meaning. But the issue is more complicated when children are given such a surname. In such circumstances it would seem appropriate for parents to change it to something innocuous – perhaps changing it to Roper or Rapier, a change which could be made simply by 'correcting' the spelling.

Also problematic is the surname Crapper, again predominantly a Yorkshire name and a variant of Cropper, plausibly an occupational name meaning harvester. Thomas Crapper, an enormously successful Victorian manufacturer of porcelain toilets, proudly displayed his name on his product, with the result that his surname has entered colloquial language with a meaning unfortunate to his relatives. Arguably this surname needs to be changed.

Tainted by association

Individuals can taint surnames. The surname Hindley is now associated with Myra Hindley and the story of the Moors murders. The surname itself is inoffensive, deriving from Hindley in Lancashire, where it is still strongly localized – indeed Myra Hindley was born in nearby Crumpsall. Yet the association with the woman frequently described in the press as 'the most evil woman in Britain' is a taint that will endure. Similarly, Sutcliffe is today associated with Peter Sutcliffe, the 'Yorkshire Ripper' convicted of 13 murders. The name is localized in Yorkshire with the result that many people who bear the name today live close to the former home of Peter Sutcliffe. The name is more common than Hindley and certainly includes prominent people who have brought credit to it, so it may be that the taint is not quite so problematic.

Humorous surnames

Names can also have a humour which may be problematic to their bearers. Yorkshire has produced a string of surnames with the ending –*bottom*, from a regional word for valley. Shufflebottom, Smallbottom and Longbottom are among the more comic surnames with this formation. Tickle (from Tickhill in Yorkshire's South Riding) and Ouch (from Asby-de-la-Zouch) surely raise a smile. Presumably people who have these surnames have heard every possible joke associated with them. Living with them may perhaps be considered character-forming.

Our amusement with names is demonstrated by the success of Russell Ash's book *Potty, Fartwell and Knob*, which was on the 2007 UK Christmas bestseller list. This volume assures its readers that Emma Royd, Gladys Friday and Herbert Sherbert are among the real names of people living in Britain.

ATTRACTIVE NAMES

Sometimes an individual can bring fame to a name. Thus Queen Victoria's reign (1837–1901) was graced with around 100 men named after the admiral Horatio Nelson, around 200 named after each of the literary giants William Shakespeare and Charles Dickens, and even a couple of dozen examples of legendary highwayman Robin Hood.

Many names are conspicuous because of a famous former bearer.

Boleyn brings to mind Ann Boleyn, second wife of King Henry VIII and who was beheaded. The link is inescapable and may be a source of pride or curiosity.

Many British Isles surnames have associations of class, which may or may not be seen as beneficial. Perhaps shockingly in 21st-century Britain there is still a statistical link between surname and social class.

SOCIAL AFFECTATION

Social affectation may be a reason to change a name. The outstanding example is the Victorian supposed 'reversion' of surnames to an earlier form where that earlier form had been misunderstood. A manuscript form of the capital letter F resembles 'ff' – confusion over this is the source of the Victorian concept of spelling surnames in a way which is simply not correct English orthography, so that a name such as Foulkes becomes ffoulkes.

Archaic spelling is found in Featherstonehaugh (for Fanshaw) – the longest single-word English surname – Cholmondeley (for Chumley), Mainwaring (for Mannering), Fiennes (for Fines), Villiers (for Villers) and Beauchamp (for Beecham), all now established as English eccentricities – indeed there have been Cholmondeleys so spelt since the early 16th century. There is even a double-barrelled example in the Surrey family of Leveson-Gower (Looson Gore). In Scotland Dalziel (Dayel), Menzies (Mingies) and Zuill (Yule) utilize the Scots orthographic convention of using a letter that resembles z for some g sounds (and additionally sometimes drops the sound entirely) and are comparable oddities.

Novelists have free range in selecting names for their characters. Occasionally these are inventions – Dickens's Micawber appears to be in this category – but usually novelists select from the existing name stock. Surnames beginning Cr– are remarkably common in the invented category (from Daniel Defoe's Robinson Crusoe to Charles Dickens's Bob Cratchitt), a phenomenon which appears to reflect an English-language aesthetic attraction to names beginning in Cr–. J. K. Rowling makes masterly use of surnames (and first names) in her Harry Potter novels. The surnames she uses fit the region, class and character of the bearer.

ACTIVITY

Taking control of your surname

▶ I hope that this book has helped you understand your surname better. I hope you feel good about your surname. Take pride in it!

▶ But remember that you are in control of your surname. If it is wrong for you or wrong for your children, then change it.

The 50 Most Common Surnames

The 50 most common surnames in England and Wales are set out in the list below. The ordering follows the Registrar General's List of 1853.

All of these names are polygenetic. Many are Welsh and of those, most of them are patronymics, and most of them 17th- or even 18th-century formations.

Allen (38) appears to be a patronymic, son of Alan. However, the relative infrequency of the first name Alan urges caution on accepting this origin. Certainly the first name existed (including for example an Alanus in the Domesday Book for Suffolk) but it had nothing resembling the popularity of other first names which gave rise to popular English surnames. It may be that for this name we have to accept that we really cannot be sure of its origin. It is common in southern parts of England: East Anglia, East Midlands, South East and South West. There is a strong cluster around Huntingdonshire, Northamptonshire, Leicestershire and neighbouring counties. It is relatively uncommon elsewhere. The cognate form Alan is associated with Scotland, particularly clusters in Orkney and Sutherland, and in Ayrshire, Dumfriesshire and Gallowayshire. It is found in Ireland mainly as a plantation name.

Baker (32) is an occupation name, one immediately recognizable today. Though widespread it is particularly characteristic of the South of England, with notable concentrations in Kent, Sussex and Surrey, and in Devon and Somerset. This may represent those areas where bakery was most developed as a village trade rather than bread being baked in each individual home.

Bennett (48) is an English patronymic. Benjamin (and its short form Ben) has long been part of the English first-name stock but never particularly common and it is surprising therefore that Bennett is quite as frequent as it is. Also surprising is use of the ending –ett (instead of –s or –son). The name is particularly common in England's West Midlands and South. The cognate form Benson is mainly found in the North of England – a complementary distribution. Neither surname is common in Wales, Scotland or Ireland.

Brown (6) and its variants including Browne and Broun is the most common surname whose origin is not known. The oft-repeated idea that it is a nickname for someone with brown hair is not credible – in a population where brown hair predominates this simply is not a distinguishing feature. In England it is most common in the North East, East Midlands and East Anglia; in Scotland it is most common in the Lowlands. The name clearly needs more investigation, and very probably has many different origins. The earliest spelling is Brun, which may suggest it is a patronymic from an English first name Brun, though the first name Brun was not common. It may be that it is on occasions a place name relating to a dozen or more settlements with an element that sounds like 'brown'. It may be an occupation name for a foot soldier or watchman who carried a brown-bill (a basic halberd which was painted brown) – and it doubtless has numerous other origins. All these origins have gravitated towards the pronunciation and spelling of the colour brown.

Carter (49) is an English occupation name, a cart maker. The name is widespread though most common in the South (particularly South East) and East Anglia. It is cognate with **Wright (13)**, a wheelwright or cart maker, with the two surnames having a complementary distribution, Wright being most common in the East Midlands and East Anglia. The cognate Cartwright is mainly found in the West Midlands.

Clark (27) is an occupation name for a clerk. In the Middle Ages this occupation was more or less synonymous with clergyman, while the term could be applied to anyone who could read and write. Clark is common in London and the East of England (particularly Essex, Leicestershire and Nottinghamshire), and is widely distributed in Scotland; it is less common in the West Midlands, South West and Wales. **Clarke (39)** is strongest in East Anglia and the Midlands, and well represented in the South West. Today the final –e is not usually sounded (as it would have been in the Middle Ages); the form reminds us of Chaucer's 'clerke of Oxford' and preserves a memory of an old pronunciation. While the trade is spelt 'clerk' – reflecting the Latin *clericus* – the surname is usually Clark(e), reflecting the pronunciation. The spelling variant Clerk is mainly found in Scotland.

Cook (40) is a trade name, often a role within the army. It is a clear example of polygenesis. The name has a wide distribution in England, particularly in the South and the East. It is less common in Wales, Scotland and Ireland.

Cooper (28) is a trade name, a barrel maker. The name is widespread in England though may derive from less than half a dozen sources. There are particular clusters in Berkshire, Hertfordshire, Norfolk and Suffolk, Wolverhampton and the East Riding of Yorkshire. The name is relatively uncommon in the South West and Wales and has a limited distribution in Scotland.

Davies (5) and **Davis (30)** are sometimes discrete names, sometimes mere spelling variants. The name is a patronymic, son of David, and has arisen independently many times. Davies is strongly localized in Wales, particularly South Wales, and is likely to be of relatively recent origin, probably as recent as the 18th century. It is likely that the –e– was originally pronounced and reflected the Welsh pronunciation of the name David; today most treat the –e– as silent. While Davis can be found in Wales it is not usually a Welsh surname – contrary to popular belief. It is found mainly in the Welsh border counties and the central South of England. The name has also arisen as a Jewish surname with a localization in the East End of London. Cognate names include Davids (parts of Wales and North West Kent) and Davidson (mainly Scotland).

Edwards (20) is a patronymic, the son of Edward. It is most commonly encountered in Wales (particularly north and central Wales) where it reflects the 18th-century adoption of surnames. However, the name is also an English patronymic of earlier origin. Within England particular concentrations include west Cornwall, Somerset, Surrey, Hertfordshire and Shropshire. It is cognate with Edwardson, predominantly a Lancashire name.

Evans (8) is a patronymic from the Welsh first name Evan, usually of recent origin and frequently formed in the 18th century. The name is strongly localized within Wales. Variants include Evanson (mainly Cheshire) and Everson (mainly Monmouthshire and

Suffolk). The initial vowel has permitted the Welsh construction *ap Evan* (son of Evan) to yield Bevan and Bevans.

Green (18) is a location name, a shortened form of precise place names including the element 'green'. It may claim to be the most typically English of the 50 most common surnames being found in the centre of England. It is unusual in the North East and Cumbria, unusual in the South West, most unusual in Wales, Scotland and Ireland, and curiously rare in Kent (though common in neighbouring Sussex). The distribution may suggest half a dozen or more separate late medieval origins, perhaps in Hampshire, Essex, Hertfordshire, Huntingdonshire, Worcester-shire, Yorkshire's West Riding and Lancashire. The name may well reward research.

Griffiths (50) is a Welsh patronymic from the Welsh first name Gruffyd. The name is of late formation, typically 17th and 18th centuries. The distribution of the name reflects its recent origin in Wales: it is found throughout Wales (and is particularly strong in South Wales) with overspill into the Welsh Border counties of England.

Hall (15) is variously a location name, a trade name and a patronymic. As a location name it should be seen as a reduced form of a place name including the element 'hall'. As a trade name it may refer to a hall worker or hall retainer. It may also be a son of Hal, Harry or Henry, cognate therefore with Halls and Henryson. Additionally it may be a reduced form of any of at least two dozen surnames beginning with Hall-. The name is common-place throughout the British Isles though there is a particular concentration in the North East of England and in the Scottish Borders. The name is less common in Wales and in South West

England. In Scotland it is unusual outside of its Borders stronghold. The name is likely to be frustratingly difficult to research, though progress could probably be made with individual families.

Harris (26) is a patronymic, son of Harry or Henry. It has an unusually strong regional localization for such a common surname. Harris is strongly associated with the South West, South East and the West Midlands. It is found in Wales also where it may be an English name brought to Wales – or may be a discrete Welsh formation, or both. The name is not common in East Anglia, the North and Scotland. **Harrison (29)** is a variant found predominantly in the North of England and the northern counties of the Midlands. It is unusual in the South West, Wales and Scotland. Harris and Harrison are therefore examples of complementary distribution.

Hill (25) is a location name. There are communities in the British Isles called simply Hill – for example, the village of Hill in Gloucestershire – but in most cases Hill is likely to be a reduced form of a name including the element 'hill'. The name is particularly strong in the South West, West Midlands and in Yorkshire. It is least common in the area where there are the fewest hills (East Anglia) and where hills are called by a different name (downs in Kent and Sussex; fells in Cumbria). The name is not common in Wales, Scotland or Ireland.

Hughes (17) is a patronymic, the son of Hugh. It is particularly associated with Wales, where it is predominantly an 18th-century formation. Within England it is likely to be much earlier. Hugh was in origin a Norman first name and some English usages may reflect a Norman surname adoption. The Welsh stronghold for the name is North Wales; in England the central South in the vicinity of Oxford is well attested. The name is relatively unusual in the South East, South West and East Anglia.

James (35) is a patronymic, both the son of James and sometimes the son of Jacob. It is most frequently encountered in South Wales where it is an example of the 18th-century Welsh adoption of surnames. However, it is widespread in the South West and West Midlands where its origin is earlier. Jameson is mainly the North of England and Scotland; Jamieson mainly Scottish.

Jones (2) is the most common surname in Wales and the second most common in England and Wales; it is widespread in Ireland also. It means simply John's son, and has arisen independently many times. Frequently it is a surname of recent origin, often as recent as the 18th century. Within Wales it is ubiquitous, though slightly more common in the north than the south. Within England it is more common in the Welsh border counties and in the West Midlands. In formation it is cognate with **Johnson (10)** (mainly northern and eastern England) and Johns (mainly South West England, though also South Wales). Also related is **Jackson (23)**, formed from Jack, the familiar nickname for John. Jackson has a distribution comparable with Johnson with particular strengths in Cumberland, Lancashire and Yorkshire. Jack is mainly found in the Scottish Highlands. The abundance of surnames based on the first name John testifies to the enormous popularity of this name in the British Isles over the last thousand years.

King (37) is variously a place name and an occupation name. As a place name it can derive from any of the many place names which include the element 'king'. As an occupation name it suggests a retainer or personal servant of a king. The name is found predominantly in the South East and East Anglia. Specific concentrations in Sussex, Dorset, Hertfordshire and Essex may possibly indicate four separate origins. Extended forms which are more obviously place names include Kingswood, Kingham, Kingsford, Kingscote, Kinghorn, Kingswell and Kingsberry.

Lee (47) is primarily an English location name from any of the many place names containing this element, which means a meadow. The name is widespread throughout England, though particularly frequent in Devonshire and the West Riding of Yorkshire, which may suggest two distinct creations in these two locations. The name is relatively unusual in Wales, Scotland and Ireland. The spelling variant Leigh has a Lancashire focus. This name has an unusual phonetic structure in the English naming system in that it is a single syllable ending with a vowel (an open syllable). While such comparable surnames as Dee and Gee do exist, this phonetic structure is most unusual. Additionally the formation of the name from the unstressed syllable of place names (for the element –lee is almost always unstressed) is a strange phonological process. In addition to its traditional English origin the name has been adopted by Romany Gypsies in Britain, traditionally pronounced with a slight aspiration at the end (almost as 'leek') where it reflects sounds in the Romany language. It is conceivable that this is the ultimate origin of most cases of this surname. The fame of the gypsy 'queen' and fortune-teller Gypsy Rose Lee has ensured that many in Britain associate the name with the Romany Gypsies. In recent years many migrants from China have anglicized a common Chinese surname Li as Lee.

Lewis (19) is a patronymic, the son of Llywelyn, a common Welsh first name. Many usages will originate in the 18th-century adoption of surnames within Wales, and it is particularly common in Wales (particularly South Wales) and the Welsh Borders. The name is relatively unusual in the East and South of England, and in Scotland.

Martin (33) is predominantly a patronymic, son of Martin, though it may also be a place name from Combe Martin (Devon) or any of the many place names including the element 'martin'. The name is widespread though three distinct localizations may be observed. In the South West it is strongest in Devon and Cornwall, in the South East in Kent and Sussex while in Scotland the name is well dispersed though with a particular stronghold in the Western Isles. The variant Martins is mainly found in Norfolk; Martyn mainly in Devon and Cornwall.

Moore (50) is a location name from the many place names with the element 'moor'. It is widely distributed within England with a tendency to occur in places where there is moorland and therefore place names with the moor element. It is well represented along the length of the Pennines. However, there are substantial numbers of this name in the South as well as in East Anglia and Essex. It is also well attested in Ireland. The name is unusual in Scotland and Wales. The spelling variant Moor is associated particularly with the North East and Cumbria, though as with Moore it has a wide distribution in England.

Morgan (36) is a patronymic, the son of Morgan, and seems to have arisen separately in Wales, Scotland and Ireland. The greatest concentration within Wales is in South Wales, particularly the vicinity of Cardiff and Monmouthshire. While found frequently throughout Wales the instances in North Wales are significantly less than in the South. In most cases it is likely to be a surname of relatively recent origin, frequently from the 18th century. Within Scotland the surname is most associated with Fife and Aberdeenshire.

Morris (34) is a patronymic, son of Maurice, and is predominantly of Welsh origin from as late as the 18th century. Outside of Wales it is common in the West Midlands and has particular strengths on the Isle of Wight and in Fife. These cases may well be earlier formations. The alternative spelling Maurice is encountered, and widely dispersed. Morrisson is mainly in the Scottish Borders and Cumberland.

Phillips (44) is a patronymic, son of Phillip, both Welsh and English in origin. As a Welsh name it is predominantly from the 17th and 18th centuries and has particular strength in South Wales. In England the name has particular strengths in Cornwall and Hampshire, which may indicate two English creations, probably earlier than the more numerous Welsh. The spelling variant Philips shows a similar distribution with the addition of Scotland. Cognate are Phillipson (mainly North East, Cumbria and Lincolnshire) and Philipson (mainly North East and Cumbria).

Parker (42) is an occupation name for a park keeper or game keeper, the person responsible for the upkeep of a noble's estates. The name is ubiquitous in England, suggesting many occasions of formation of this surname in widely scattered locations. It is unusual in Wales, Scotland and Ireland.

Price (43) is a patronymic from the Welsh *ap-Rhys*, son of Rhys. While common throughout Wales it has an unusually clear focus in the old counties of Brecknockshire and Radnorshire. The name is relatively unusual in Scotland and Ireland while in England it has a concentration within the Welsh Border counties. The name is a 17th- or 18th-century Welsh patronymic. Unusually the most common patronymic form from this Welsh first name is based on the Welsh language structure *ap-Rhys* not the English 'Rhys's son'; it may well be that the triple sibilant in Rhys's son discouraged this formation. Rhys is mostly found in the South of Wales; Reece in Monmouthshire and Herefordshire.

Roberts (9) is a patronymic from the first name Robert. It is particularly well attested in Wales (and there most strongly in the north) and is likely to be in most cases of relatively recent formation, probably 18th century. The name is also widely distributed in England, where it is likely to be of much earlier origin, perhaps 14th or 15th centuries. In Scotland the name is found as Robertson, associated particularly with Perthshire, the East Coast and Shetland. **Robinson (11)** is similarly a patronymic from the first name Robert (and more rarely Robin). It is most often found in the North of England and the East Midlands.

Shaw (46) is a location name deriving from the many place names which include the element 'shaw'. It is common in the North of England and in the Midlands (particularly the northern counties of the Midlands). The West Riding of Yorkshire is an area where it is particularly well represented. It is widespread in Scotland. The name is unusual in the South of England and East Anglia, as well as Wales and Ireland.

Smith (1) is well known as the most common English surname. It is also number 1 in Scotland and number 5 in Ireland. Spelling variants are predominantly Victorian in origin, including Smyth (mainly in Ireland), Smithe, Smythe, Smithes and even Smijth and Psmith, the last popularized by novelist P. G. Wodehouse. It is an occupation name from the trade smith – typically a blacksmith, but also on occasions a goldsmith or silversmith. The tendency for the occupation smith to pass from father to son encouraged the establishment of this surname. Surprisingly even this most common of surnames has a clear regional distribution, being most common in the English Midlands and East Anglia. It is rarely found in Wales, in South West England and in rural areas of North West England. Within Scotland it is common in Aberdeenshire, Angus, Fife and Shetland, and relatively uncommon elsewhere. The surname has also been favoured by Gypsy families. Today there are around half a million Smiths in the British Isles alone.

Taylor (4) is an occupation name and arose independently many times. Curiously the spelling Tailor is uncommon. It may be that the forms – ay– and –ai– were regarded as calligraphic differences rather than as true spelling differences, with –ay– perceived as more formal, and therefore appropriate for someone's name. This widespread name is most common in England, particularly in and around Birmingham, Manchester and Lincoln, while in Scotland it is particularly common in and around Aberdeen. The name is relatively unusual in the South West, Wales and the Lowlands of Scotland.

Thomas (7) is a patronymic, the son of Thomas. It is frequently an 18th-century Welsh formation, being particularly common in South Wales, though commonplace throughout Wales. In England it is most strongly associated with the Welsh Borders and the South West. It is cognate with **Thompson (21)** (most common in the North of England) and Thomson, usually from Scotland. Both Thompson and Thomson are likely to be older than Thomas, at least in most cases.

Turner (24) is an occupation name for a wood-turner or carpenter. It is widely distributed within England, much less common in

Scotland, Wales and Ireland. While the name is surely poly-genetic, it is a candidate for a restricted number of adoptions. There are discrete focuses in the West Midlands and in East Anglia. It may be possible to identify a limited number of early Turner families from whom all Turners are descended.

Walker (16) is a trade name, the trade of a walker being that of a fuller or wool cleaner, someone whose job was to treat wool within a walk-mill or full-mill so that it could be spun. The process is known from antiquity though mills dedicated to the process developed in England and Scotland around the 13th and 14th centuries, and the surname may be dated to this period. With the mills came people who specialized in this one stage (rather than the whole process from shearing to finished garment) and who could reasonably be called walkers. The distribution of the name reflects the hill country of northern England where sheep were commonplace in the Middle Ages (sheep grazing was much less common then in the south of England) with the surname following the crest of the Pennine Chain and being well represented in Cumbria. In Scotland the name similarly follows the medieval distribution of sheep grazing, being mainly Lowland – sheep in the Highlands are largely a development from the second half of the 18th century. Fuller – from the same occupation – is favoured in East Anglia and the South East.

Ward (31) is an occupation name – ward is a watchman or gate-keeper. The name is late medieval, a time when such occupations were common, and arose separately many times. The name is most common in the West Midlands, North West and East Anglia – and unusual in Wales, Scotland and Ireland.

Watson (45) is an English patronymic, usually the son of Wat or

Walter. This first name was more common in the late Middle Ages than it is today; the short form Wat is best known from Wat Tyler, leader of the Peasants' Revolt. Watson is most common in the North East, East Midlands and Cumbria, and is widely spread within Scotland. The name is unusual in Wales and South West England. The cognate form Watts is found particularly in the South of England while Wats is found both as a Welsh patronymic and in parts of South England (particularly Berkshire). Wattson is predominantly an Oxfordshire form.

White (22) is a trade name, that of white smith or silver smith. Widespread in England, it nonetheless has a focus within the South of England and is particularly strong in Hampshire, Wiltshire and Dorset. Whyte is almost entirely a Scottish spelling variant for a name found mainly on the East Coast: Fife, Angus and Aberdeen-shire. It may be an anglicization of several names from outside the British Isles, including Dutch Witt, German Weiss and French Blanc, and is found among Jewish and Huguenot communities in the British Isles. The oft-repeated assertion that this name is a nickname in origin is hard to support. While circumstances might be imagined where an individual is described by this name, it is hard to see why it should become hereditary.

Williams (3) is strongly associated with Wales, the Welsh borders and South West England. It means simply the son of William and has arisen many times. Within England the surname often has medieval origins; within Wales it is usually more recent, frequently as recent as the 18th century. In formation it is cognate with Williamson, most frequently encountered in Scotland and the North of England, and **Wilson (12)** widely distributed in the North of England and Scotland and particularly common in Cumbria and the Scottish Lowlands.

Wood (14) is a location name from a multitude of places which contain the element 'wood'. It is particularly common in Yorkshire and Lancashire, in Kent, Sussex, Surrey and Essex and in the Scottish Borders. It overlaps with Woods, particularly common in East Anglia, Surrey and Lancashire.

Wright (13) is an occupational name from the trade a wheelwright (wheel maker). The trade frequently passed from father to son, facilitating the adoption of the name as a surname. The name is particularly common in the East Midlands and East Anglia – and relatively rare in the South and Wales. This distribution may reflect the geographical distribution of the nouns 'wheelwright' and 'cartwright' (cart maker) describing essentially the same trade – from cartwright is Cartwright (mainly West Midlands) and **Carter (49)** (mainly South and East Anglia) with the names forming a complementary pattern with Wright.

General Index

Aaron, 136, 167–8
Alfriston, 88
America, 151–5
Anglo-Saxon, 23, 52, 72
Antrim, County, 120–1
Aramaic, 22
Armstrong, Neil, 65
Ash, Russell, 182
Ashkenazim, 133–4
Australia, 30, 146–50

Balliol, John, 106
Barnstaple, 26
Battle Abbey Roll, 78–9
Battle of Culloden, 108, 111
Battle of Hastings, 23, 72–9
Battle of the Standard, 55, 64
Bayeux Tapestry, 73
Beatles, The, 90
Becket, Thomas, 158
Birmingham, 156
Black Death, 156
Bonnie Prince Charlie, 111
Brian Boru, 115–16
Brown, 23, 146
Burns, Robert, 113
Bute, Isle of, 108
by-name, 8

Camden, William, 43

Canada, 151–5
canting, 81–2
caveman/woman, 172
Celtic, 115, 165
census, 12
Channel Islands, 78, 128–31
Chief Herald of Ireland, 83
China, 11
clans, 111
coats of arms, 80–4
cohanim, 168
College of Arms, 83
common surnames, 13
compurgation, 96
Cornish, 67–8, 91
Cornwall, 91–3
Council of Forfar, 104
Court of Lord Lyon, 83
Cromwell, Oliver, 90
Cromwell, Thomas, 88

Danelaw, 50
databases, 4
David I, 64–5, 77, 105–6
Defoe, Daniel, 183
Denmark, 180
Derry/Londonderry, County, 121
dialect dictionaries, 38
Dickens, Charles, 52, 84–5, 184
dictionaries, 4, 12–14, 20

Index of Surnames